WORLD WAR II
THE END OF WORLD WAR II:
THE JAPANESE SURRENDER

WORLD WAR II

THE END OF WORLD WAR II:
THE JAPANESE SURRENDER

MASON CREST

Mason Crest
450 Parkway Drive, Suite D
Broomall, PA 19008
www.masoncrest.com

Printed and bound in the United States of America.

First printing
9 8 7 6 5 4 3 2 1

ISBN: 978-1-4222-3898-1
Series ISBN: 978-1-4222-3893-6
ebook ISBN: 978-1-4222-7908-3
ebook series ISBN: 978-1-4222-7903-8

Produced by Regency House Publishing Limited
The Manor House
High Street
Buntingford
Hertfordshire
SG9 9AB
United Kingdom

www.regencyhousepublishing.com

Text copyright © 2018 Regency House Publishing Limited/Christopher Chant.

PAGE 2: *The light carrier Belleau Wood was hit by a kamikaze aircraft but survived.*

PAGE 3: *U.S. troops survey Japanese gun emplacements after they had captured the tiny island of Tarawa, in the Gilbert Islands group, in an immensely costly battle between November 20 and 23, 1943.*

RIGHT: *The mushroom cloud rises over Hiroshima after the U.S. atomic bombing of this port city on August 6, 1945.*

PAGE 6: *A Chinese soldier guards a line of American P-40 planes.*

CONTENTS

KEY ICONS TO LOOK FOR:

 Words to Understand: These words with their easy-to-understand definitions will increase the reader's understanding of the text, while building vocabulary skills.

 Sidebars: This boxed material within the main text allows readers to build knowledge, gain insights, explore possibilities, and broaden their perspectives by weaving together additional information to provide realistic and holistic perspectives.

 Educational Videos: Readers can view videos by scanning our QR codes, providing them with additional content to supplement the text. Examples include news coverage, moments in history, speeches, iconic sports moments, and much more!

 Text-Dependent Questions: These questions send the reader back to the text for more careful attention to the evidence presented here.

 Research Projects: Readers are pointed toward areas of further inquiry connected to each chapter. Suggestions are provided for projects that encourage deeper research and analysis.

 Series Glossary of Key Terms: This back-of-the-book glossary contains terminology used throughout the series. Words found here increase the reader's ability to read and comprehend high-level books and articles in this field.

OPPOSITE: Marine Pfc. Douglas Lightheart (right) cradles his 30-cal. machine gun in his lap, while he and his buddy Pfc. Gerald Churchby take time out for a cigarette, while mopping up the enemy on Peleliu Is. September 14, 1944.

National World War II Memorial

The National World War II Memorial in Washington, D.C., is dedicated to the 16 million people who served in the American armed forces during World War II. The memorial also honors the 400,000 who gave the ultimate sacrifice for their country. Those who supported the war effort at home are honored too. The memorial symbolizes World War II as the defining event of the 20th century.

The memorial is situated on a 7.4-acre (3-hectare) site. It was created by designer and architect Friedrich St. Florian who won a national open competition for its design. The construction of memorial took place between 2001 and 2004 and then opened to the public on April 29, 2004; its official dedication took place a month later, on May 29. It was commission by President Clinton in 1993 who authorized the American Battle Monuments Commission (ABMC) to establish a World War II memorial in the Washington, D.C. area.

The memorial is an elliptical shaped plaza built around a splendid fountain and pool, with water jets in its center. Built in a semi-classical style, there are 56 granite columns forming a semi-circle around the perimeter. Each one is designed to symbolize the unity of the states, federal territories, and District of Columbia. The entry walkway is flanked by ornate balustrades decorated with 24 bronze bas-reliefs.

At the mid point of the plaza there are two pavillions decorated with bronzes, featuring Baldachins, American Eagles, and World War II Victory Medals. The pavillions represent the Atlantic and Pacific theaters.

At the western end of the memorial is a curved Freedom Wall bearing a field of 4,048 golden stars, each of which stands for 100 American military deaths in the war. Before it lies a granite curb inscribed "Here we mark the price of freedom."

Throughout the memorial are inscribed quotations from eminent military and political figures, including Gen. (later Pres.) Dwight D. Eisenhower, U.S. Presidents Franklin D. Roosevelt and Harry S. Truman, Col. Oveta Culp Hobby, Adm. Chester W. Nimitz, Gen. George C. Marshall, and Gen. Douglas MacArthur.

The National World War II Memorial is located at the east end of the Reflecting Pool on the Mall, opposite the Lincoln Memorial and west of the Washington Monument. The memorial is maintained by the U.S. National Park Service, and receives almost 5 million visitors each year. It is open 24 hours a day and is free to all visitors.

WORLD WAR II
Chapter One
ASCENDING THE LADDER OF THE SOLOMAN ISLANDS

Their defeats of 1942 and early 1943 in Papua and Guadalcanal worried the Japanese high command severely, for in this area now lay the greatest danger of an Allied breakthrough into the Southern Resources Area so vital for Japan's continued ability to wage the war and prosper economically once it was over. The decision was therefore taken to reinforce the area strongly. The key to the region's defenses was Rabaul, on New Britain, and it was to this that men and matériel were sent to replace those lost in the Papua and Guadalcanal battles. From Rabaul these additional resources were to be allocated as the local commanders saw fit, mostly to the garrisons in the **Huon Gulf** in north-eastern New Guinea and in the Solomon Islands chain as far to the south-east as New Georgia Island. The Japanese had

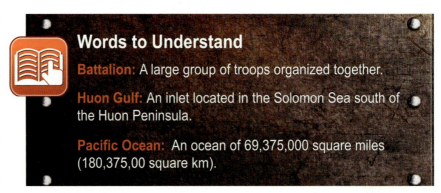

Words to Understand

Battalion: A large group of troops organized together.

Huon Gulf: An inlet located in the Solomon Sea south of the Huon Peninsula.

Pacific Ocean: An ocean of 69,375,000 square miles (180,375,00 square km).

no joint command structure, and it thus depended on the good sense of commanders whether or not the army and navy acted in cooperation. In this area, however, it was good: overall command was exercised by Vice-Admiral Jinichi Kosaka, commanding the 8th

Area Army of Lieutenant-General Hitoshi Imamura. The 8th Area Army controlled two formations, Lieutenant-General Hotaze Adachi's 18th Army in New Guinea, and Lieutenant-General Iwao Matsuda's 17th Army in the Solomon Islands. Given that this threatened area was the key to the naval-controlled defense perimeter on which Japan's fate hung, Admiral Isoroku Yamamoto, the commander-in-chief of the Combined Fleet, kept a watchful eye on the situation from his headquarters in Truk, far to the north in the Caroline Islands.

The general Allied strategy for the area had been fixed in July 1942, and following the defeat of the Japanese attempts on Port Moresby and Guadalcanal, the forces of General Douglas MacArthur's South-West Pacific Area were ready to begin the drive on Rabaul. The South Pacific Area was dissolved, Vice-Admiral William F. Halsey's naval forces in the area becoming the 3rd Fleet, which was allocated to MacArthur's overall command. The drive on Rabaul was to have two axes. Supported by the aircraft of Lieutenant-General George Kenney's U.S. 5th Army Air Force, Lieutenant-General Walter Krueger's U.S. 6th Army was to advance up the coast of New Guinea and then invade the western end

of New Britain before making the final assault on Rabaul. At the same time, Halsey's forces were to "island-hop" through the Solomon Islands toward the north-west and thus in the direction of Rabaul. The one major problem that had to be overcome was a command and related logistical one: although under MacArthur's strategic command, Halsey was still dependent on Admiral Chester Nimitz's **Pacific Ocean** Areas for men and matériel. MacArthur and Halsey worked very smoothly as a team, however, which overcame many of the problems that might have defeated two less tolerant commanders.

The advance through New Guinea was finally made possible by the capture of Buna on January 22, 1943. Some preparatory movements had already been carried out, the most important of these being the airlift to Wau, about 30 miles (50km) south-west and inland of the major Japanese coastal garrison of Salamaua, of an Australian brigade from Lieutenant-General Edmund F. Herring's New Guinea Force. The brigade established a forward base and threatened the Japanese as MacArthur put the finishing touches to the main assault plans and readied his forces. To make the Japanese think that his drive would be straight along the coast, a **battalion** of the U.S. 32nd Division was

landed at Nassau Bay on June 30, just to the south of Salamaua, and this battalion, together with the Australian 17th Brigade from Wau, now threatened Salamaua from the west and south. At the same time the U.S. 158th Infantry Regiment took Trobriand Island, and the US 112th Cavalry Regiment took Woodlark Island, both of these lying north-east of the south-eastern tip of Papua. This completed the clearance of Japanese garrisons in Papua between Buna and Milne Bay undertaken in October and November 1942.

OPPOSITE: *A 6.1-inch (155-mm) howitzer of the U.S. Marine Corps in action on one of the Solomon Islands group. Throughout the war with Japan, the U.S. forces possessed significantly greater numbers of heavy artillery.*

ABOVE RIGHT: *A tank landing ship of the U.S. Navy disgorges supplies for the men of the U.S. Marine Corps somewhere in the Solomon Islands group.*

RIGHT: *The wreckage of a Mitsubishi G4M "Betty" twin-engined bomber, again somewhere in the Solomon Islands group. Japanese warplanes were notable for their very long range, but this capability was bought only by the sacrifice of protective features, such as armor for the crew and vital systems, and protection for the fuel tanks.*

The Japanese were considerably shaken on September 4, 1943 when the Australian 9th Division of the New Guinea Force, now commanded by General Sir Thomas Blarney, landed east of the main base of Lae in the Huon Gulf. A day later the U.S. 503rd Parachute Regiment dropped at Nazdab, inland of Lae, thus completing the isolation of the garrison. The airborne "airhead" was swiftly reinforced by the Australian 7th Division, which was airlifted from Port Moresby. The Allied forces at Salamaua and Lae now attacked simultaneously, Salamaua falling on September 12 and Lae on September 16. While the Australian 9th Division advanced around the coast, the Australian 20th Brigade was shipped around to Katika, where it landed on September 22, cutting off the garrison of Finschhafen, which fell on October 2.

After its capture of Lae, the Australian 7th Division had moved up the Markham river valley, inland of the Saruwaged and Finisterre ranges of mountains, and then crossed into the Ramu river valley as it made for Madang, which fell to the Australian 11th Division on April 1944 24. Overland advances and landings from the sea completed the isolation and

destruction of other Japanese garrisons on the Huon peninsula during the same period. Of the 10,000 Japanese troops in the area, half had been killed, the other half dispersed into the cruel jungle of the region.

While the Australians were mopping up on the Huon peninsula, the U.S. 6th Army had secured a toehold on the

western end of New Britain. The 112th Cavalry Regiment made a diversionary landing at Arawe, on the south coast of New Britain on December 15, 1943, and 11 days later the 1st Marine Division came ashore at Cape Gloucester at the western tip of the island. The division quickly secured a beach-head with two airfields, after 1,000 Japanese had been killed in a hard, four-day battle.

Halsey's forces had also been active during this period as they began to move up the "ladder" of the Solomon Islands group. After a brief pause to rest and reorganize after their defeat of the Japanese on Guadalcanal, the Americans resumed with the capture of the Russell Islands, just to the north-west of Guadalcanal, by the 43rd Division on February 21, but this was only a preliminary move. The basic U.S. plan was now to bypass the main Japanese garrisons, concentrating instead on a series of outflanking movements to secure key air bases and so isolate the Japanese garrisons. This would avoid heavy losses and, it was hoped, neutralize the Japanese bases.

The first major step up the ladder was New Georgia Island, where Japan's main air bases in the Solomons were located. As an initial move, the island of Rendova, just off New Georgia, was

taken as an artillery base on June 30. The main landings went in near Munda on July 2, the assault forces being the 37th and 43rd Divisions with U.S. Marine support. Overall control of the ground force was exercised by Major-General John P. Hester, later to be replaced by Major-General Oscar W. Griswold. The Japanese were commanded by

OPPOSITE ABOVE: U.S. infantryman and a Sherman medium tank combine to flush out Japanese defenders on the island of Bougainville late in 1943.

OPPOSITE BELOW: Landing craft, carrying men of the 3rd Marine Division, approach the coast of Bougainville for a largely unopposed landing around Cape Torokina on November 1, 1943.

ABOVE: U.S. front-line medical personnel train under tropical and jungle conditions typical of the Solomon Islands group. The location is Arundel Island off New Georgia.

Lieutenant-General Noboru Sasaki, who led his men ably, so the fighting was extremely bitter, and at first it was the raw U.S. troops who came off the worse in desperate struggles in the jungle. The 25th Division had to be committed on 25 July, and after regrouping and resting his forces, Griswold finally took Munda airfield on August 5. The back of the Japanese resistance had been broken, and all organized opposition ended on August 25. There had been heavy casualties on each side.

On August 15, meanwhile, a U.S. regimental combat team (about the equivalent of a British brigade) had leapfrogged past Kolombangara, which had an important airfield, to land on Vella Lavella. After building an airfield the Americans were withdrawn and replaced by the New Zealand 3rd Division, which was able to crush the last Japanese resistance by the middle of September. The Japanese on Kolombangara, realizing their impossible situation, evacuated the island, and the central rung of the Solomon Islands was in Allied hands by October 7.

The last major rung before New Britain was the large island of Bougainville, which had several airfields. To distract the Japanese, the 3rd Marine Parachute Battalion landed on nearby Choiseul Island on October 27. The battalion was evacuated a week later, having accomplished its task. Also on October 27, the New Zealand 8th Brigade Group landed on Treasury Island, which was quickly secured as an advanced base for the Bougainville operation. Moving forward from here, the 3rd Marine Division landed at Empress Augusta Bay on Bougainville on November 1. At first, Japanese resistance was light, and a naval base and airfields were soon operational within a beach-head 10 miles (16km) wide and 5 miles (8km) deep. Japanese opposition then grew, and by the end of the year the perimeter had hardly been advanced. The only real chance the Japanese had had of evicting the Americans from Bougainville had been in the Battle of Empress Augusta Bay on November 2, but the radar-equipped ships of the U.S. task force proved too powerful for the

Consolidated B-24

Long-range air power projection in the Pacific theater rested primarily with the Consolidated B-24 four-engined bombers of the U.S. Army Air Forces. This aircraft is seen in 1944, during a raid on Koror, one of the main islands of the Palau Islands group.

steadily east, and on March 6 the 1st Marine Division had made a forward landing at Talasea on the Willaumez peninsula. It was now decided to halt the U.S. forces where they were and henceforward to contain the Japanese. Gradually, Australian forces assumed the task of keeping a watch on the Japanese for the rest of the war, freeing MacArthur's U.S. divisions for further operations. The successful neutralization of Japanese strength in the area also allowed the 3rd Fleet to be returned to Nimitz's control in June.

The Japanese perimeter had been horribly dented, but the authorities in Tokyo decided that the western end of New Guinea could still be held by Lieutenant-General Jo Iimura's 2nd Area Army, based in Hollandia, just over the border in occupied Dutch New Guinea. Here a great complex of airfields and supply dumps had been built, but there were few troops in the area. Most of the 18th Army's surviving men, some 65,000 strong, were based in the areas of Wewak and Madang.

In an action of some genius and great risk, MacArthur decided to bypass the 18th Army and go for Hollandia itself, even though this was beyond the range of Kenney's aircraft. Although

Japanese force, which lost a cruiser and a destroyer, and had most of its other vessels damaged. To complete the ascent up the Solomon Islands ladder, on February 15, 1944 the New Zealand 3rd Division took Green Island, to be used as the location of a forward airfield for attacks on Rabaul.

Realizing that the actual conquest of New Ireland and eastern New Britain would be extremely costly, the Allies had by now decided merely to cut them off, leaving them to "wither on the vine" in their isolation. So it was necessary, finally, to take the islands north of New Britain and New Ireland to complete the encirclement. Accordingly, MacArthur's forces moved on the Admiralty Islands and Halsey's on the St. Matthias Islands. A reconnaissance of Los Negros in the Admiralties on February 29 met little opposition and the 1st Cavalry Division quickly moved in to secure the island by March 23. A landing was also made on Manus on March 15. Halsey's 4th Marine Division landed unopposed on Emirau in the St. Matthias Islands group, moving swiftly forward to Mussau. New

Britain and New Ireland, with their great bases at Rabaul and Kavieng, were now cut off. On New Britain, the 1st Marine and 40th Divisions had been moving

Nimitz had lent him Vice-Admiral Marc A. Mitscher's Fast Carrier Task Force to provide air cover, MacArthur decided to land forces at Aitape, at the same time as the Hollandia landings, to secure the airfields there. The Aitape landing could be covered by aircraft based at Saidor, and once Aitape's airfields were in U.S. hands, the Hollandia landings could be covered by Kenney's aircraft, freeing Mitscher for other tasks.

While the Australians were pressing into Madang, far to the rear, MacArthur's two landings were committed on April 22. The 24th and 41st Divisions landed on each side of Hollandia, which fell on April 27; in two days a pair of reinforced regiments secured Aitape. In both places the fighting had been very heavy, and although the U.S. forces lost only 550 killed, Japanese dead totaled more than 14,000, the other Japanese in the area having been dispersed into the jungle. MacArthur's forces now advanced in bounds along the coast, taking Sansapor island, at the western end of New Guinea, on July 30, and bringing the New Guinea campaign to an end.

Blarney's Australian forces, meanwhile, had been fighting to a halt a last-breath offensive by the 18th Army in the area of Wewak and Aitape. This was finally crushed on August 5.

Now that Japan's defensive perimeter had been breached, MacArthur was able to turn his attention to the Philippines group.

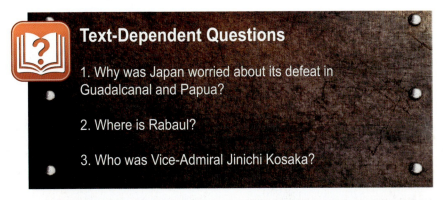

Text-Dependent Questions

1. Why was Japan worried about its defeat in Guadalcanal and Papua?

2. Where is Rabaul?

3. Who was Vice-Admiral Jinichi Kosaka?

Research Projects

Why were the Solomon Islands considered significant during World War II?

OPPOSITE: Wounded U.S. soldiers on a beach in New Georgia wait for transport out to a hospital ship or a warship equipped with major medical facilities.

ABOVE: Men of the U.S. Marine Corps on New Georgia, which was assaulted by forces of the U.S. Army and USMC from June 30, 1943.

WORLD WAR II

Chapter Two
THE CAMPAIGNS IN THE PACIFIC AND BURMA

The forces of Vice-Admiral William F. Halsey's U.S. 3rd Fleet had made the first island-hopping operations in the course of their advance up the Solomons' ladder, but the technique could not be used there to full effect. In the Central Pacific, however, there was more than ample scope for such tactics, for in the vastnesses of this ocean, with Japan's bases scattered over a multitude of little islands and atolls separated from each area by hundreds of miles of open sea, the steadily growing strength of the U.S. Navy could be used to transport and support the formations of the U.S. Army and U.S. Marine Corps to overwhelm the lesser Japanese garrisons with local superiority of forces. Having fewer ships, the Japanese could not match the U.S. forces' level of strategic mobility, and the U.S. leadership believed that this should make it possible for its forces to close gradually on Japan without encountering the need to tackle major bases until the later stages of the campaign.

While General Douglas MacArthur was firmly in favor of a methodical approach to Japan via New Guinea and the Philippine Islands group, Admiral Ernest J. King, the chief of naval operations, and Admiral Chester W. Nimitz, commanding the Pacific Ocean Areas, favored a more indirect approach across the Central Pacific to take Formosa or part of the Japanese-held mainland of China. In the thinking of the U.S. Navy, the Imperial Japanese empire would then be cut in two, separating Japan's industry and population from the raw materials and food which they obtained from the south. This, the U.S. Navy believed, would greatly weaken Japan and so facilitate the final assault on the Japanese home islands should this prove necessary. The grand strategic question of which plan was better did not have to be answered until 1944, so until then there was room

for both the U.S. Army and the U.S. Navy to advance in their own areas, MacArthur in the South-West Pacific and Nimitz across the Central Pacific. The U.S. armaments factories were by now delivering matériel in quantities so vast that there was ample for MacArthur

and Nimitz, even though the war against Japan in general possessed a lower priority than the theaters in which the Germans were being fought.

To a great extent Nimitz was helped by MacArthur's efforts: feeling that the South-West Pacific constituted their

was shot down by Lockheed P-38 Lightning long-range fighters operating from Henderson Field on Guadalcanal. This was yet again a direct result of U.S. cryptanalysis, in this instance of the itinerary of Yamamoto's tour of inspection. Yamamoto was succeeded by Admiral Mineichi Koga, who lacked the strategic genius and popularity of his predecessor.

Throughout the first nine months of 1943, Nimitz built up his forces and planned his campaign. With the return of Vice-Admiral Halsey's 3rd Fleet from the Solomon Islands in June, Nimitz was able to assemble the greatest naval force ever created, which constantly grew until the end of the war. The main striking force was built around the large numbers of fast fleet and light aircraft carriers emerging from U.S. yards at a remarkable pace, supported by modern and modernized battleships as well as large numbers of cruisers, both heavy and light, and exceptionally capable fleet destroyers. When commanded by Halsey, this force was known as the 3rd Fleet, which became the 5th fleet when commanded by Vice-Admiral Raymond A. Spruance. The main offensive element of this was the Fast Carrier Task Force, led by Vice-Admiral Marc A. Mitscher. Other air support came from the U.S.

greatest threat, the Japanese had responded by sending to this theater the best of their air units from the separate army and navy air forces, with the result that the Central Pacific garrisons were left with mere handfuls of aircraft and indifferent crews. Even the good aircrews were being killed in large numbers, and their replacements, moreover, were

decidedly inferior. The Japanese suffered yet another blow with the death of Admiral Isoroku Yamamoto, commander-in-chief of the Combined Fleet, on April 18, 1943, when his aircraft

OPPOSITE: After taking Tarawa and other islands of the Gilbert Islands group late in 1943, the U.S. forces moved north-west to tackle the primary Japanese garrisons in the Marshall Islands from January 30, 1944. Here the U.S. flag flies from a shattered coconut palm after the island of Kwajalein had been taken on February 1–4, 1944.

ABOVE: U.S. infantrymen during the fight for Guam, the most southerly of the larger islands in the Mariana Islands group, taken between July 21 and August 10, 1944.

RIGHT: A Japanese tank is knocked out by the 77th Infantry Division at Yigo, Guam.

WW II in Color
Battle for Burma

Army's 7th Air Force, commanded by Major-General Willis H. Hale, operating from the Ellice Islands group. For landing operations, Nimitz had some 100,000 men, plus all their transports and the supply facilities necessary for far-flung operations.

The first objectives for the Central Pacific drive were the Gilbert and the Marshall Islands groups, whose capture would provide real estate for the airfields required for the air forces which would provide support for the next step forward. These two large groups of tiny atolls were to be taken in two phases: November 1943 for the southern part (Makin, Tarawa, and Apamama in the Gilberts), and late in January and early in February 1944 for the northern part (Eniwetok, Kwajalein, and Majuro in the Marshalls). The landing forces had little idea what they were up against, for every majo islet fringing each atoll had been heavily fortified, and was defended by first-class troops.

Makin and Tarawa were to be assaulted on November 20, and for a week before had been saturated with bombs and naval gun fire which, unknown to the attackers, made almost no impression at all. Deep within their coral, concrete and coconut-log bunkers, the Japanese were safe from anything but a direct hit, but waited for the inevitable assault. Makin fell to the 165th Regiment of the 27th Division on December 23, but its 600 defenders had held up the Americans for far too long to suit Major-General H.M. "Howling Mad' Smith, commander of the V Amphibious Corps. All of the 250 combat troops were killed, and the 100 prisoners were all Korean laborers.

By comparison with Tarawa, however, Makin was a simple task. Rear-Admiral Keiji Shibasaki had some 4,700 seasoned troops, and formidable defenses including 8-inch (203-mm) guns and 400 pillboxes and bunkers. Reconnaissance had not revealed the presence of an inner reef, on which most of the landing craft had been grounded, forcing the men of the 2nd Marine Division to wade hundreds of yards through a curtain of fire. Their losses were appalling. The marines were then trapped on the beaches, and 1,500 of the 5,000 men landed had become casualties by nightfall. Reinforcements in the next two days suffered comparable losses, but gradually the marines forced the

defenders back. The last pocket of Japanese resistance was overwhelmed on November 23, by which time the Americans had lost 985 men killed and 2,193 wounded. The Japanese lost all but about 100 taken prisoner, of whom only 17 were combat soldiers. In the long run, however, the Central Pacific forces benefited from their experience on Tarawa, having learned the tactics necessary and seen the need for landing craft that could crawl over reefs and

OPPOSITE: Japanese prisoners of war on Guam. It was only in the fighting for the Mariana Islands that the U.S. forces began to take more than the smallest handfuls of Japanese prisoners.

ABOVE: A U.S. flamethrower in action on Kwajalein atolls in the first days of February 1944.

onto the shore. These emerged as LVTs (landing vehicles tracked), which were armored and tracked amphibious personnel carriers and tanks. The southernmost of the Gilbert Islands, Apamama, fell quickly on November 21.

The Japanese Combined Fleet had no aircraft and could only lie impotently at anchor in the Truk lagoon.

Kwajalein was defended by some 8,000 men under Rear-Admiral Monzo Akiyama. The 7th Division landed and overran the island during February 1–4. The 4th Marine Division took other islands in the group. The lessons of Tarawa had been well understood, and the Americans suffered only 372 dead and about 1,000 wounded out of some 41,000 men landed. All but 230 of the Japanese defenders were killed. Majuro had been occupied on January 30, but the islets of the Eniwetok atoll were to prove another tough nut to crack. On

February 17 two battalions of the 22nd Marine Regiment came ashore on Engebi, at the north of the atoll, and met little resistance; but on February 19 two battalions of the 106th Regiment met very determined and fierce resistance when they landed on Eniwetok atoll itself. Only after two days of heavy fighting was this little area of coral declared secure. Two battalions of the 22nd Marine Regiment encountered similar opposition on Parry Island, when they landed on February 22, and it took a day's hard fighting to crush the Japanese. This sterling defense had been mounted by Major-General Yoshima Nishida's 1st Amphibious Brigade, an experienced unit some 2,200 strong. The Americans suffered some 339 dead, but all the Japanese were killed. Flamethrowers proved particularly effective in assaulting bunkers.

Truk

Truk, in the Caroline Islands group, was a vital center for the protection of the Japanese defense perimeter in the central Pacific, and the Combined Fleet was often based in its great lagoon. Truk was therefore a primary objective of attacks by U.S. warplanes. On February 17–18, 1944 Vice-Admiral Marc A. Mitscher's Task Force 58 (five fleets and three light carriers with battleship and cruiser support) attacked Truk, where the lagoon accommodated some 50 merchantmen, protected by three light cruisers and eight destroyers as well as 350 land-based aircraft.

was able to lay its plan in adequate time, and Nimitz detached about one-third of his forces to protect the Aleutians. Hosogaya managed to outmaneuver Rear-Admiral Robert Theobald's force, however, and twice shelled Dutch Harbor, much to the embarrassment of the Americans, before retiring westward to establish bases on Kiska and Attu on June 6 and 7 respectively. Air support for the garrisons of Kiska and Attu was provided by land-based aircraft operating out of Paramushiro, the most northerly of the Japanese-owned Kurile Islands, that lay to the south of the tip of Kamchatka.

There was no compelling military need for Nimitz to eject the Japanese from his Northern Pacific Area other than injured U.S. pride, caused by Japanese occupation of American soil. Nevertheless, the decision to do this was taken in 1943. On March 26, Hosogaya was convoying reinforcements to the islands with two heavy and two light cruisers, as well as four destroyers, when he fell in with Rear-Admiral Charles McMorris's force of one heavy cruiser, one light cruiser and four destroyers. The Battle of the Komandorski Islands was a

Mitscher's carriers had meanwhile struck at Truk on February 17–18. Although Koga managed to escape with the Combined Fleet, the U.S. carrierborne aircraft sank 200,000 tons of merchant shipping and destroyed 275 aircraft on the ground. Koga retired from Truk as a permanent base in favor of anchorages in the Philippine Islands group. On April 1 Koga was killed in an accident, and was succeeded as commander-in-chief of the Combined Fleet by Admiral Soemu Toyoda.

Late in May 1942, as part of their deception plan for the Midway operation, the Japanese had sent a force north against the Aleutian Islands group off the coast of Alaska. The task of Vice-Admiral Boshiro Hosogaya's Northern Area Force of two light aircraft carriers, seven cruisers and 12 destroyers was to establish bases in the Aleutians, in the islands toward the western end of the chain. Once again as a result of cryptanalysis, the USA

OPPOSITE: *U.S. marines in the fighting for Garapan on the western side of Saipan Island, in the Marianas group, during mid-June 1944.*

ABOVE: *Men of the U.S. Marine Corps land on Saipan on June 15, 1944. The vehicle (left) in an amphibious tractor (amtrak), the type of armored and tracked landing craft and assault vehicle which proved so successful in the Pacific campaign's later operations, especially when fitted with a tank turret carrying a short-barrel howitzer for close-support fire.*

long-range gun duel in which the U.S. cruiser *Salt Lake City* was crippled and the Japanese cruiser *Nachi* were very seriously damaged. As the Japanese closed in for the kill, however, three of the U.S. destroyers also closed in for a torpedo attack, forcing Hosogaya to turn away for home.

Rear-Admiral Thomas Kinkaid, commanding in the North Pacific, ordered Rear-Admiral Francis Rockwell to land the 7th Division on Attu to clear out the Japanese. This landing went in on

May 11, and after 18 days of fighting in appalling terrain and bitter weather Attu was declared secure. Only 29 of the 2,500 Japanese defenders were captured, and the Americans lost 561 dead and 1,136 wounded. On August 15 a joint Canadian and American force landed to fulfil a similar function on Kiska, but found that the Japanese had gone. The 4,500 defenders had in fact been lifted off a fortnight earlier, when the Japanese high command realized that the sacrifice of the garrison would serve no purpose.

immensely slow and difficult, and the men and animals were more than decimated by the region's diseases.

There was also the oddness of engaging in combat with the Japanese, who at times would attack with phenomenal courage and great tactical skill, but at others preferred to dig themselves into bunkers, impervious to all but the heaviest artillery shells, holding the bunkers until the very last individual Japanese had been killed. Even a reversion to the methods of a previous century and digging in a 3.7- inch (94-mm) howitzer to blast the bunker at close range over open sights failed, although it did pave the way to the bunker-busting techniques, using tanks and guns, that were perfected at a later date.

For six weeks the Indian 14th Division, reinforced with brigade after brigade, tried unsuccessfully to break through. Then, when the men of the attackers were exhausted, the Japanese counter-attacked, the Allied resistance broke, and the whole force, badly shaken, returned to India.

Another threat to the Japanese appeared 600 miles (965km) away to the extreme north of Burma. The CAI had been created by Stilwell from the remnants of the Chinese divisions he had led on foot out of Burma in 1942, together with new units flown from China. These had been collected at Ramgarh, in Bihar, and trained on U.S. lines under Stilwell's direction. The training was undertaken on a "conveyor-belt" system, in which squads of hundreds of men learned to aim and fire their weapons on a strict schedule with a minimum of frills. These squads were then grouped in companies and battalions for training under their own Chinese officers. The battalions were all-

THE SECOND ROUND OF THE WAR IN BURMA

In 1943 the Allies strongly desired to take the war back to the Japanese, but lacked the means to do so in a major way, despite the fact that the Japanese position, at least in theory, was weak. The "Greater East Asia Co-Prosperity Sphere" had expanded with great speed and to a very large extent, and was, in theory, ripe to be pricked and deflated. The Japanese armed forces were fully committed to one major land campaign in China and another in the Pacific, so only a small fraction of the Japanese army faced the British-Indian forces to the west in Burma, Lieutenant-General Joseph W. Stilwell's Chinese Army in India to the north, and the many Chinese armies to the east.

Unfortunately for the Allies, the best Indian divisions had already been dispatched to the Middle East, and those available in India were low in morale and required training for jungle warfare. The majority of the Chinese armies were useless, and only the Chinese Army in India (CAI) was in any position to fight in any effective manner. Stilwell was determined to get to grips with the Japanese as soon as possible, but the British generals were equally determined to resist taking the offensive until they had trained their men to fight the Japanese effectively. In this respect the dismal defeat of the first offensive in the Arakan coastal region of Burma had strengthened this resolve. In January 1943 three brigades of the Indian 14th Division were advancing with great difficulty along the Arakan coast toward the port of Akyab. The Japanese resistance was light, but it was the terrain which provided the greatest difficulty: mountains, roadless jungles, mangrove swamps and tidal creeks made movement

Chinese, and Stilwell commanded them via advisers and liaison officers at the regimental and divisional levels. Stilwell's greatest problem was the Chinese system of dual command, ordered by Generalissimo Chiang Kai-shek, who interfered constantly by signal, always on the side of urging caution and obstructing Stilwell's orders for offensive action. Stilwell's task was to drive the Japanese south and so clear the way for a new road through northern Burma for the movement of munitions and supplies to the Chinese, now cut off by land and sea and being expensively supplied by air. With the newly-organized 38th Division leading, the CAI started south on February 28, 1943.

The Japanese were content at this time to remain on the defensive in Burma, but this was a defense of the active type. In northern Burma Lieutenant-General Shinichi Tanaka's 18th Division was deployed in a 100 mile (160km) long series of outposts from a point to the south of Ledo to Fort Hertz, but Tanaka nonetheless made local attacks and administered some sharp jolts to the intruders. Such was the prestige of the Japanese and their aggression that the British-Indian outpost garrisons were soon retreating north and the Chinese 38th Division of General Sun Li-jen was halted. Primarily the military adviser and chief of staff to Chiang Kai-shek, Stilwell felt he had to take command of the CAI in the field, and after a great deal of persuasion managed to get it creeping forward in December: even when compared with the rest of Burma, the Patkai hills and the Hukawng valley were appallingly difficult areas in which to live, let alone stage an offensive.

Tanaka was deterred from exploiting his easy successes in the north by the unexpected intrusion of the Indian 77th Brigade of British and Gurkha troops into northern Burma from February 8, 1943. This had infiltrated, largely undetected, across the Chindwin river, which was then the line of contact between the British in Assam and the Japanese in what was no ordinary raid. Brigadier Orde Wingate had been ordered to study the possibilities of

warfare behind the enemy lines by Field-Marshal Sir Archibald Wavell, the commander-in-chief in India. On the basis of the guerrilla methods he had already tested in Ethiopia, Wingate had already evolved the concept of "long-range penetration" using scattered company-strong columns controlled by radio and supplied from the air. These columns could move through the jungle, using it as a covered approach for attacking vulnerable Japanese rear areas.

Operation Longcloth had been intended as part of a combined British and Chinese offensive, but when this was cancelled Wingate persuaded Wavell to let him go ahead alone, in order that his new strategy and novel methods of training troops on guerrilla lines could be fairly tested in battle. By no purely objective military criterion could this first Chindit experiment be judged a success, for all the courage and self-sacrifice shown by the troops, who accepted that no sick or wounded could hope to be evacuated. All went fairly well at first: some successful skirmishes were fought against the Japanese and the railway to the north was cut. Wingate, whose

intentions were never clear, even in his own mind, then rashly moved into an area where his force was in grave danger of being trapped. He extricated part of it by the expedient of abandoning all his heavy weapons and animals, and dividing his men into small parties. However, part of his force did not receive the order to withdraw and failed to return: the survivors suffered terrible hardships from fatigue, starvation, and disease. Of the original 3,000 men, some 800 failed to return and of the survivors only 600 were fit for further active operations. But when the public learned that for three months a commando-type force had been at large and on the rampage behind the lines of the apparently invincible Japanese, there was an enormous uplift in morale.

Wingate's message was simple and its effects were far-reaching. For the British it was that the Japanese could be defeated, and for the Japanese that the jungle could be penetrated and the Chindwin front was now vulnerable. The Japanese now began to think less about the defense of Burma and more about attack, and began the planning that was to lead them to Imphal and Kohima.

WORLD WAR II

Chapter Three
CENTRAL PACIFIC SUCCESS AND BATTLES IN THE PHILIPPINES

With the Gilbert and Marshall Islands groups taken, and the Aleutian problem being solved, Admiral Chester W. Nimitz, commander-in-chief of the Pacific Ocean Areas and of the Pacific Fleet, focussed on his next Central Pacific objective, the **Mariana Islands** group, in the spring of 1943. These are of rock rather than coral, and offered a different set of problems for the assaulting land forces. The three main islands to be taken were Saipan, Guam and Tinian, and it was decided to attack them in that order. The primary strategic objective of the undertaking was the capture of land areas large enough for the creation of the bases

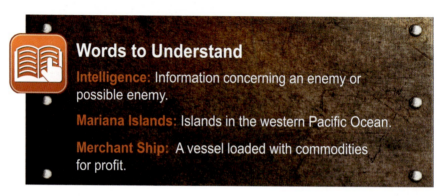

Words to Understand

Intelligence: Information concerning an enemy or possible enemy.

Mariana Islands: Islands in the western Pacific Ocean.

Merchant Ship: A vessel loaded with commodities for profit.

from which the long-range bombing of Japan could be effected, using the new Boeing B-29 Superfortress four-engined

heavy bomber. Working on the basis of prewar maps and aerial reconnaissance photographs, U.S. Army Air Force

LEFT: The battle for Peleliu, in the Palau Islands group, lasted from September 15 to November 25, 1944, and cost the U.S. forces 2,336 men killed and 8,450 wounded, while the Japanese lost 10,695 men killed and 202 taken prisoner. This is the wreckage of a Japanese tank, it turret ripped off by an internal explosion.

OPPOSITE ABOVE: Mail call for men of the U.S. Marine Corps on Tinian Island in the Marianas group on July 30, 1944, just two days before the end of organized Japanese resistance on the island.

OPPOSITE BELOW: The M1 carbine was developed as an intermediate-power weapon for the use of second-line troops and those needing to carry other equipment, but its light weight, small size, and adequate short-range stopping power soon made it attractive to men fighting at close quarters with the Japanese. These are men of the 22nd Marine Regiment, three of whose battalions took Parry Island in the Kwajalein atoll complex on February 22–23, 1944.

engineers calculated that they could build an enormous complex of airfields on the islands, sufficient to allow the war to be taken to Japan in a major way.

The targets in the Marianas were softened on June 11–12 by a visit from Vice-Admiral Marc A. Mitscher's Fast Carrier Task Force, and some 200 Japanese aircraft and many **merchant ships** were caught and destroyed in this initial sweep. Vice-Admiral Richmond K. Turner's V Amphibious Force of 530 ships, and the 127,000 men of the III and V Amphibious Corps, commanded by Major-Generals H.M. Smith and Roy S. Geiger respectively, arrived off the islands on June 15, after steaming from the rendezvous point of Eniwetok. Commanding in the Marianas was Vice-Admiral Chuichi Nagumo, commanding the Central Pacific Area Fleet, which had no ships. Nominally in command of the land forces, constituted by the 31st Army, was Lieutenant-General Hideyoshi Obata. At the time of the American invasions Obata was away in the Palau Islands group, so command of the ground forces was undertaken by the senior commander on each island.

After a feint attack on Mutcho Point, on the center of Saipan's west coast, by reserve regiments of the V Amphibious Corps, the real attack was delivered on each side of Afetna Point, farther to the south, by Major-General Thomas E. Watson's 2nd Marine Division and Major-General Harry Schmidt's 4th Marine Division to the north and south respectively. Both landings were strongly contested by the forces of Lieutenant-General Yoshitsugo Saito. Although American **intelligence** had estimated that there were 20,000 Japanese on Saipan, Saito had 25,469 army troops and 6,160 naval personnel. By June 18 the Americans had reached the eastern coast of the island before turning north and south to crush the halves of the Japanese defense into the ends of the island. The 27th Division, commanded by Major-General Ralph C. Smith, had been committed on June 17, which did little to speed up the pace of the U.S. advance.

The Japanese southern pocket at Nafutan Point was soon contained by a

single battalion of the 27th Division and was destroyed on June 28, the rest of the division having been ordered to line up between the two marine divisions for the northward advance, scheduled for June 23. Fighting to a different set of tactical precepts, the army division soon fell behind the more probing marine divisions, and Howling Mad Smith precipitated a major inter-service argument, by replacing Ralph Smith with Major-General George W. Griner.

The problem was not Ralph Smith, but rather the differences in tactical doctrine that existed between the U.S. Army and U.S. Marine Corps. After heavy fighting, by the end of the month the three divisions had reached a line running roughly across the island from Garapan on the west coast. The 2nd Marine Division was pulled out of the line as the advance continued to move into a narrower part of the island. By July 7 the Japanese position was desperate, and Saito issued orders for a last suicidal counterattack from Makunsha. Beaten back with great loss by the 27th Division, this marked the end of the road for the Japanese. Although U.S. progress had been slowed by the absence of tactical air support, as a result of Mitscher's departure for the Battle of the Philippine Sea with his Task Force 58, the Japanese were finally crushed by July 9. Rather than surrender, hundreds of civilians killed themselves by jumping off the cliffs at Marpi Point. The Japanese troops suffered some 27,000 dead, but 2,000

were taken prisoner, while the U.S. forces suffered some 3,126 dead and 13,160 wounded, most of them marines. Both Saito and Nagumo committed ritual *seppuku* to avoid capture.

Guam was next on the objective list, and was to be taken by the 3rd Marine and 77th Divisions, commanded by Major-Generals Allen H. Turnage and Andrew D. Bruce respectively, as well as the 1st Provisional Marine Brigade, led by Brigadier-General Lemuel C. Shepherd, of Geiger's III Amphibious Corps. Command of the Japanese forces on this largest of the Marianas had been entrusted to Lieutenant-General Takeshi Takeshima, the commander of the 29th Division, although only one regiment of the division was present on the island. In all, Takeshima had some 13,000 soldiers, and some 5,500 naval personnel were commanded by Captain Yutaka Sugimoto. It should be noted that Obata had hurried back from the Palau Islands on learning of the U.S. landings on Saipan, but had been able to proceed

no farther than Guam. He left the command arrangements as they were, but when Takeshima was killed on July 28, assumed command of what was left of the defense.

The two marine formations landed north and south of the Orote peninsula, on the western side of the island, during July 21, with the 77th Division following the 1st Provisional Marine Brigade later in the day. Fighting was again severe, but

ABOVE: *The U.S. Army's 77th Infantry Division fought on Guam Island in the Marianas group. This photograph was taken on July 26, 1944 as the division advanced across to and then north along the eastern side of the island.*

OPPOSITE: *Ground crew and brother pilots salute a pilot about to take off for a kamikaze mission in his obsolescent Mitsubishi A6M Reisen Zero fighter, carrying heavier-than-standard bombs.*

not as hard as it had been on Tinian. The halves of the corps linked up in a good beach-head on July 22 and then turned north to the capital of Agana and on to the tip of the island at Ritidian and Pati Points. As on Saipan, the Japanese defended with great courage, launching counterattacks when they were able, but were slowly driven back. The end of the organized resistance came on August 10 on Mount Machanao, at the north-west tip of the island. U.S. casualties totaled 1,919 dead and 7,122 wounded, but the Japanese total was as usual far higher at 17,300 dead and 485 taken prisoner.

This left only Tinian to be secured, the invasion of which was scheduled for July 24. The assault was undertaken by the 2nd and 4th Marine Divisions, commanded by Watson and Major-General Clifton B. Cates respectively, of the V Amphibious Corps, now commanded by Major-General Harry Schmidt since the elevation of H.M. Smith to the post of Commanding General, Fleet Marine Force, Pacific. The 27th Division was in reserve after its hard time on Saipan. Although the senior commander on the island was Vice-Admiral Kakuji Kakuda, commander of the 1st Air Fleet, tactical command was exercised by Colonel Kaishi Ogata of the 50th Infantry Regiment. Ogata had some 4,700 army personnel, with Captain Goichi Oya leading the 4,110 personnel of the 56th Naval Guard Force.

While the 2nd Marine Division launched a feint towards Tinian town in the south-west of the island, the 4th Marine Division landed on two tiny beaches on the north-west tip of Tinian, early on July 24, meeting only relatively light resistance. The 2nd Division then arrived from its feint, landing across the same beaches. The two divisions fought off an ineffectual night counterattack, and on the following day moved off to the south, the 2nd Division on the left and the 4th Division on the right. Progress was steady, and by July 28 the two divisions had taken half the island. The Japanese were gradually penned up in the south-east of the island, and the final assault went in on July 31, with all organized resistance ending on August 1. As usual, Japanese losses had been very

heavy (6,050 men killed and 235 taken prisoner) compared with the marines' loss of 290 dead and 1,515 wounded.

With the three islands secured, the engineers arrived with their equipment to start work on the great airfield complexes needed for the air side of a three-pronged strategic offensive against Japan: air attacks on industry from bases in China and the Marianas; submarine attacks on shipping, especially tankers to starve Japan of raw materials and oil; and the combined land and sea offensive to retake Japan's conquests and invade the home islands if necessary. B-29 operations from the Marianas started on October 28 with a raid on Truk, but soon great numbers of these strategic heavy bombers were winging their way to Japan from the Marianas.

With his Central Pacific offensive complete, Nimitz could turn his attention once more to the debate on the best route by which to approach the Japanese home islands. Both he and MacArthur, the main protagonists of the two different schools of thought, attended the conference in Hawaii during July, at which President Franklin D. Roosevelt made his decision. The fall of the Marianas and their defeat in the Battle of

the Philippine Sea had the result, in Japan, of bringing about the fall of Lieutenant-General Hideki Tojo's government on July 18, to be replaced by a slightly more realistic one under General Kumaki Koiso.

THE BATTLE OF THE PHILIPPINE SEA OR THE "GREAT MARIANAS TURKEY SHOOT"

In March 1944 the Americans set in motion their operation to capture the Marianas so that airfields could be built for the Boeing B-29 Superfortress heavy bombers which were to attack and cripple industry and transportation in the Japanese home islands. But the Marianas were also a useful staging post for Japanese ships and aircraft in transit between the home islands and the south-west Pacific, and therefore featured strongly in Japanese strategic thinking. The Japanese naval forces were commanded by Admiral Soemu Toyoda, with the 1st Mobile Fleet led by Vice-Admiral Jisaburo Ozawa and comprising five battleships, nine carriers and 13 cruisers. Toyoda was certain that the next American thrust would be to the south, so he and Ozawa planned to use a decoy force to lure the Americans from the

Marshall Islands group toward Ulithi in the Caroline Islands group or alternatively to the Palau Islands, from which they could be attacked by aircraft. But somehow the Japanese ships had to be kept out of reach of the U.S. carrierborne warplanes. The Americans had a fast carrier force of seven fleets and eight light carriers, carrying 700 fighters and nearly 200 bombers. In addition, the U.S. invasion forces would be covered by escort carrier groups, carrying more than 300 fighters and bombers. The Japanese could muster more than 600 aircraft in the Marianas and western Carolines and, furthermore, were able to reinforce them by flying in fresh aircraft from the home islands via Iwo Jima.

To preserve their carriers the Japanese therefore planned to stay out of the reach of U.S. carrierborne aircraft but within the range over which their own carrierborne warplanes could attack: they would hit the U.S. carriers which, according to the plan, would already have been damaged by Japanese land-based aircraft, land on Guam to refuel and rearm, and attack the U.S. carriers for a second time on their way back to their carriers. But the Japanese aircraft were basically inferior to those of the Americans at the technical level, and were flown, moreover, by completely indifferent crews, whereas the American air groups were composed of experienced and confident aircrews, with hundreds of replacements on the way.

On June 6, 1944 Vice-Admiral Mitscher's Task Force 58 left the lagoon of the Majuro atoll in the Marshall Islands, and five days later its warplanes made the first sweeps over Guam, Saipan, and Tinian. The Americans reported enormous successes, but their intelligence had underestimated the numbers of shore-based aircraft, making them mistaken in their belief that they had wiped out the Japanese defenders. A heavy bombardment of Saipan started on June 13, followed by the landing of 20,000 men two days later. As soon as the Japanese were certain that the attack was not a diversion, Ozawa was given the order to sail. On June 13 he left Tawitawi in the Sulu Islands archipelago,

ABOVE LEFT: *U.S. aircraft carriers come under Japanese air attack during the Battle of Leyte Gulf.*

LEFT: *Left essentially naked of aircraft and aircrews as a result of the Combined Fleet's earlier losses, the fleet carrier Zuikaku was part of the Japanese decoy force in the Battle of Cape Engano, within the Battle of Leyte Gulf, and was sunk on October 25, 1944. The other three carriers, which the Japanese lost in the same battle, were the light carriers Chitose, Chiyoda and Zuiho.*

OPPOSITE: *A Japanese destroyer explodes after a bomb from an attacking U.S. warplane had penetrated into its forward magazine and detonated the stored ammunition.*

with the giant battleships *Yamato* and *Musashi* among other ships. Unfortunately for him, a lurking U.S. submarine reported the departure of the fleet, while another spotted it emerging from the San Bernadino Strait into the Philippine Sea on the evening of June 15.

Admiral Raymond A. Spruance, commanding the U.S. 5th Fleet, was kept informed of the expected attack, and wisely postponed the landing on Guam to allow the transports to be kept well clear of the battle area. Leaving only a force strong enough to cover the Saipan invasion, Spruance concentrated his ships about 180 miles (290km) to the west of Tinian, for he was determined not to be lured away until he knew the whereabouts of the main Japanese fleet. Ozawa, for his part, was confident that his plan was going well, for he had kept out of range of the U.S. carrierborne warplanes, and his own aircraft had reported the position of the U.S. force. On the night of June 18–19 Ozawa divided his force into an advance guard under Vice-Admiral Takeo Kurita, with four battleships and three medium-sized carriers, keeping the main force of six carriers under his own command. He hoped that Kurita's force, some 100 miles (160km) ahead of him, would be able to draw the greater weight of the U.S. attack, so leaving his five carriers intact for a decisive blow against Spruance.

Thereafter matters began to go awry for the Japanese. During the evening of June 18 Ozawa imprudently broadcast an appeal to the shore-based air forces for a maximum effort on the following day: U.S. high-frequency direction-finding stations picked it up, passing a fairly accurate estimate of Ozawa's position to the 5th Fleet during the same evening. Spruance reacted with his customary caution and refused to close at once, but he did order TF 58 to strike against the Guam air forces to make certain that Ozawa would get no support from that quarter.

On the following morning Ozawa's carriers began the first strikes against the 5th Fleet, but just after the Japanese flagship *Taiho* had flown off aircraft for the second wave she was torpedoed by the submarine *Albacore*. The brand-new

30,000-ton carrier was in no danger of sinking from a single hit but the blast had ruptured her aviation fuel lines, the ventilation system allowing lethal fumes to permeate the entire ship. All that was needed was a spark to send a series of explosions ripping through the ship; to make matters worse, an improperly refined grade of oil was being carried as furnace fuel, which also produced inflammable vapor. When it exploded it blew the bottom out of the engine room, and most of the 1,700 men aboard *Taiho* died with her in the holocaust.

Ozawa suffered another disaster about three hours later when the submarine *Cavalla* put three torpedoes into another of his carriers, the *Shokaku*, which soon sank to leave Ozawa with only four carriers. Meanwhile, the air attacks on the 5th Fleet were not going as well as hoped. Most of the bombers and torpedo-bombers had been detected on radar and intercepted before they got within range of their targets. But the later strikes gave the Americans a close shave.

The battleship *South Dakota* was hit by a 551-lb (250-kg) bomb and a damaged torpedo-bomber crashed into the side of her sister, *Alabama*; two carriers were damaged by bombs and several more escaped damage by good luck and frantic maneuvering. More than 50 Japanese aircraft had got through the screen, and would have produced impressive results in the hands of more experienced pilots.

The Mobile Fleet launched four strikes, totalling nearly 400 aircraft with the shadowing reconnaissance aircraft. Losses ran to 243 aircraft, a further 30 or more returning with serious damage. By the following day the surviving seven Japanese carriers had only 68 fighters and 32 bombers still operational. The aircraft based on Guam had been wiped out, with 52 destroyed on the ground, 58 shot down and many more seriously damaged. In contrast, the U.S. Navy had lost only 30 aircraft, six of them by accident rather than in action. But the most grievous loss of all was in aircrew. Over 400 Japanese died, whereas the

Americans were able to save 17 out of the 44 aircrew shot down.

The Americans found that the scale of attacks had swamped their fighter-direction capability, and it became hard to distinguish between friendly and hostile radar contacts. Under the stress of protracted combat the U.S. pilots tended to forget the need for radio discipline, and the controllers had difficulty in getting through top-priority messages concerning enemy attacks.

Early in the afternoon of June 19 Ozawa turned north-west to refuel his ships, but Spruance contented himself with recovering his aircraft and continued on a westerly course. Spruance had no accurate idea of Ozawa's movements, but did not order the night search which might have produced some information. Next morning, at first light, reconnaissance revealed nothing, and a special long-range search was sent too far north of Ozawa's position to achieve anything of importance. Nothing was known until mid-afternoon, by which time the Mobile Fleet was 300 miles (480km) away. This meant that any attack would require the returning

aircraft to land in darkness, and few of the U.S. pilots had been trained in this difficult technique. But Mitscher did not hesitate to order an attack, and by 4:30pm 85 Grumman F6F Hellcat fighters, 77 Curtiss SB2C Helldiver dive-bombers, and 54 Grumman TBF Avenger torpedo-bombers were airborne.

The U.S. warplanes reached the Mobile Fleet in fading light, and between 18:40 and 19:00 committed themselves in a series of coordinated attacks. The defending fighters, about 40 Mitsubishi QA6M Reisen Zero machines, fought with skill and determination: they managed to hold off the Hellcats and broke into the large U.S. formations. In spite of being outnumbered the Zeros succeeded in shooting down six fighters and 14 bombers, but were so heavily outnumbered that they lost 25 of their own number. The carrier Hiyo was hit by aircraft from the Belleau Wood and sank. Ozawa's flagship, the veteran Zuikaku, was set on fire by several bomb hits, and the Junyo was hit by a single bomb from one of the Lexington's aircraft. The smaller carriers, Chiyoda and Ryuho, were also damaged, as were the battleship

Haruna and the heavy cruiser Maya, but Ozawa was able to extricate his force and return to Okinawa without further loss.

The Americans paid a heavy price for making their attack at such a distance. The desperately weary pilots and observers, many of whom had been in combat throughout the day, had to fly back as night fell. As their fuel gauges approached the "empty" mark, pilots looked for a friendly warship near to which they could ditch. For those who managed to land on their carriers there were still the hazards of a night-landing, and many crashes resulted. Mitscher ignored the risk of giving his position away to any lurking Japanese submarines by switching on the deck landing lights in order to give his aircrew a chance of survival. Some 80 aircraft were lost through lack of fuel or landing accidents, but the escorting destroyers were fortunately able to rescue 160 out of the 200 aircrew forced to ditch in the sea.

The 5th Fleet was angry and frustrated by its failure to destroy Ozawa's entire Mobile Fleet, and many felt that Spruance's caution had robbed them of a decisive victory. The disaster of the Taiho went unnoticed, and if the U.S. Navy had known that three and not two fleet carriers had been sunk, feelings might not have run so high. On the Japanese side there was no such doubt about the decisiveness of the victory, and Ozawa offered his resignation. Another large part of Japanese air power had been wiped out with virtually nothing to show for the sacrifice.

The Philippine Sea and the Mariana Islands were now under U.S. control, a prerequisite for the invasion of the Philippine Islands group, and the Japanese defensive perimeter had been badly breached. The performance of the U.S. Navy's submarines had been remarkable, not only in the combat role when sinking two carriers, but in the less glamorous job of reporting the passage of the Mobile Fleet at two vital moments. In retrospect the only doubt about the Battle of the Philippine Sea can be over Spruance's failure to locate Ozawa on the night of June 19. Had that happened it would have been possible to have struck earlier on the following day.

THE BATTLE OF LEYTE GULF

As with the U.S. landings in the Marianas, the Japanese planned a bold response to any U.S. invasion of the Philippine Islands group, which in the event was a descent on Leyte on October 20, 1944. But this time there was a difference, for the Japanese leadership had finally begun to admit the possibility of defeat, and was planning a final gamble in a desperate attempt to retrieve Japan's fortunes.

The plan had been carefully constructed by the staff of Admiral Soemu Toyoda, commander-in-chief of the Combined Fleet, and involved almost all of the surface fleet as well as the surviving carriers, with a decoy force to lure away a sizeable part of the U.S. fleet and three other surface forces to smash their way through to the invasion beaches to destroy the invasion fleet with gunfire. The Japanese forces were therefore divided into four parts. The Main Body or Northern Force, under Vice-Admiral Jisaburo Ozawa, comprised the fleet carrier *Zuikaku*, the three small carriers *Chitose*, *Chiyoda* and *Zuiho*, two battleships converted into hybrid battleship carriers but without aircraft, three cruisers, and eight destroyers. Force A or Center Force, under Vice-Admiral Takeo Kurita, comprised the super-battleships *Yamato* and *Musashi*, the battleships *Nagato*, *Kongo* and *Haruna*, 12 cruisers and 15 destroyers. Force C or the Southern Force was divided into a Van Force under Vice-Admiral Shoji Nishimura and a 2nd Striking Force under Vice-Admiral Kiyohide Shima, and comprised the old battleships

OPPOSITE: *Rocket-firing landing craft saturate the Japanese beach defenses with high explosive just before men of the U.S. 6th Army start to land during October 20, 1944 on the eastern side of Leyte Island, the first of the Philippine Islands group to be liberated from the Japanese.*

RIGHT: *Supported by a mass of warships, U.S. landing craft and amtraks are lined up ready for the run into the assault beaches on Leyte Island on October 20, 1944.*

Yamashiro and *Fuso*, four cruisers, and eight destroyers.

Although the Southern Force had the same objectives, its two admirals were responsible to different superiors, a division of command which was to prove disastrous. The Northern Force had the task of steaming south from Japan toward the Philippines, with the sole object of luring Admiral William F. Halsey's Fast Carrier Task Force away from the invasion area in Leyte Gulf: Ozawa's task was thus to accept casualties in order to make certain that the other three groups could have a free hand in sinking the invasion fleet. Kurita's Center Force was to steam from Borneo through the San Bernardino Strait to Leyte Gulf, where it would link with the two halves of the Southern Force which had fought their way through the Surigao Strait between Leyte and Mindanao. This massive concentration of ships would then fall on the huge fleet of transports lying helpless off the invasion beaches.

For once the U.S. Navy's submarines did not detect the Japanese movements, and Ozawa's departure from the Inland Sea on October 20, went unnoticed, with the result that he was not yet functioning properly as a decoy. But submarines did

spot Kurita's force passing Palawan three days later, and the *Darter* succeeded in sinking his flagship, the heavy cruiser *Atago*, and damaging her sister the *Takao*. The *Dace* sank a third heavy cruiser, the *Maya*, giving the Japanese plan a poor start. Part of Shima's force was also sighted and that night Kurita's force was seen in the Mindoro Strait. However, the watching submarines still failed to report the whereabouts of Ozawa's decoy force. The U.S. Navy acted on the assumption that such major Japanese forces must be on their way to Leyte Gulf through the Surigao Strait, with Halsey disposing his forces accordingly. Vice-Admiral Marc A. Mitscher's Task Force 38 was divided into four groups, and three of these were stationed 125 miles (200km) apart in the area to the east of the Philippine Islands. Task Group 38.3, under Rear-Admiral Forrest C. Sherman, was the most northerly, located off central Luzon, with four carriers, two battleships and four light cruisers. Task Group 38.2, under Rear-Admiral G.F. Bogan, had three carriers, two battleships and three light cruisers, and was off the San Bernardino Strait. To the south, off Samar island, was Task Group 38.4 under Rear-Admiral R.E.

Davison, with two fleet carriers, two light carriers, one heavy cruiser, and one light cruiser. Halsey's flagship, the battleship *New Jersey*, was with Bogan's Task Group 38.2 to the north. This was the most powerful fleet assembled during the entire war, but it could still be caught off balance if the intentions of the Japanese were misunderstood.

At dawn on October 24 Halsey ordered air searches from Lingayen, on the west side of Luzon, down to the north of Mindanao, but not to the north or north-east. The result was that the Central and Southern Forces were sighted by noon, making for the San Bernardino and Surigao Straits, but the Northern Force was still undetected. Halsey prudently ordered his three task groups to concentrate, taking the precaution of ordering the fourth group, Task Group 38.1, under Vice-Admiral J.S. McCain, back from its refueling position 500 miles (800km) to the east. In the meantime, however, TG 38.3 was attacked by shore-based aircraft, which succeeded in damaging the light carrier *Princeton*. While other ships were trying to help the blazing carrier, Ozawa launched his aircraft against them, but the raw pilots had great difficulty finding their targets. Although Ozawa

had only about 30 aircraft left after his fruitless attack on TG 38.3, this hardly affected the plan, his purpose being to attract attention to himself. At last Halsey ordered a search to the north, the direction from which the attack had come, but of course Sherman's task group was under heavy air attack and could not comply until about 2:00pm. It was 4.40pm before the American reconnaissance aircraft found the Northern Force, by which time it was 190 miles (305km) away to the north-north-east, too far away for an attack.

Kurita's Center Force was all the while under heavy attack from U.S. carrierborne aircraft. After incessant attacks the 64,000-ton *Musashi* was hit by some 20 torpedoes and slowly became unmanageable. The heavy cruiser *Myoko* was also badly damaged, but Kurita's force had not otherwise been hit. Nevertheless, he decided to reverse course for a while to escape further attacks and to wait until he received confirmation that the Americans had swallowed the bait. Halsey obliged by concluding that the Center Force had been so severely mauled as to be no longer a threat to the 7th Fleet, which was covering the invasion in Leyte Gulf. Acting on that assumption he declared

that Ozawa's force was the main Japanese force, ordering all his battleships and carriers to make pursuit. The trap had been sprung. The U.S. staff organization now compounded the error. At 3:12pm on October 24 Halsey sent a message to his forces indicating his intentions of forming a new task force of battleships and carriers to stop Kurita's Center Force off the San Bernardino Strait. This was only an intention, but it was read by Vice-Admiral Thomas C. Kinkaid of the 7th Fleet and others to mean that the force had already been formed, leading them to assume that the exit was guarded. In fact no ships at all were guarding the strait, and there was nothing standing between Kurita and the invasion fleet.

To the south, Nishimura's force was heading steadily toward the Surigao Strait, where the 7th Fleet had been alerted to the danger. The old battleships under Rear-Admiral Jesse B. Oldendorf, which had been detailed for shore bombardment in association with the landings, were warned at 12:00pm to prepare for a night engagement. Unfortunately, the battleships had only a small proportion of armor-piercing ammunition, and had already used half their high-explosive projectiles against the Japanese beach defenses. The cruisers and destroyers were also low on ammunition. But Oldendorf's captains remained confident they could hold their own in a night action as a result of their efficient radar and fire-control systems.

Just after 10.36pm on October 24 the Van Force of the Southern Force was detected by a Mindanao PT-boat patrol, followed by the Rear Force at a distance of about 30 miles (50km). The PT-boats attacked as the two Japanese forces steamed up the strait, firing 34

LEFT: *General Douglas MacArthur and staff land at Palo beach on Leyte Island during October 20, 1944. As he had promised in 1942, he and his men had returned to liberate the Philippine Islands.*

OPPOSITE: *Men of the U.S. 6th Army land on Leyte Island.*

U.S. naval fleet during the Battle of Leyte Gulf

torpedoes, but only one hit was obtained on a light cruiser. By 2:00am Shima and Nishimura were still progressing well, but came under destroyer attack about an hour later. This attack damaged the *Fuso* and *Yamashiro*, each of which was struck by a single torpedo. Neither ship suffered major damage, but three of the four Japanese destroyers were sunk or badly damaged. A second destroyer attack was then committed, its torpedoes hitting the *Yamashiro* for a second time and sinking a destroyer. At 3:49am the battleship *Fuso* blew up after a succession of torpedo hits, breaking in two and drifting off to the south. The flagship *Yamashiro* seemed indestructible, for she took another two torpedoes at about 4:11am without stopping. The U.S. were using classic destroyer tactics, in which they completely shattered the Japanese formation, leaving only the *Yamashiro*, the cruiser *Mogami* and a single destroyer to face Oldendorf's six battleships. In fact the destroyer attacks were still in progress as the head of the Japanese line came into range of the U.S. battleships and cruisers, which were crossing the "T" of the Japanese advance and could therefore all pour a withering fire onto the *Yamashiro*. The Japanese battleship was soon ablaze from stem to stern. The *Mogami* escaped by a miracle, but the *Yamashiro* capsized at 4:19am, taking most of the crew down with her. Seeing the destruction that had overtaken the other ships, Shima turned about in an attempt to avoid the same fate, losing

only one destroyer in the process, but when daylight came his ships were subjected to heavy air attacks, which at last accounted for the *Mogami*.

While Nishimura was being annihilated in the Surigao Strait battle, Kurita seemed to be in sight of victory. Not until 4:12am on October 25 was any check made as to whether or not the San Bernardino Strait was guarded, and even then an answer from Halsey was not available until 6:45am. Then the escort carriers learned the news that they were practically within gun range, for at 6:55am the *Yamato* opened fire on them with her 18.1-inch (460-mm) guns at a range of 29,965 yards (27400m). Despite the fact that these small carriers were almost defenseless, with their aircraft carrying only light bombs and their hulls lacking all armor protection, they fought heroically and ultimately successfully against Kurita's ships. The screening destroyers sacrificed themselves to save the carriers, and only the *Gambier Bay* was sunk, at a cost of three U.S. destroyers. Baffled, the Japanese withdrew to the north, just as it seemed to the Americans that they were going to brush through the limited opposition they could put up, and so get to the invasion fleet. Kurita's change of plan

was probably caused by the strain of incessant attack, coupled with his lack of adequate intelligence. He was aware that Nishimura's forces had been wiped out, and was also worried about his fuel supply. But whatever the cause, it was a golden opportunity thrown away, having been the finest Japanese chance since Pearl Harbor to inflict a major defeat on the U.S. Navy. After more aimless maneuvers, Kurita withdrew at midday.

Kurita was harried by U.S. carrierborne aircraft, but it was Ozawa who was the target of Halsey's full wrath. The aircraft of the U.S. carriers sank the carriers *Zuikaku*, *Zuiho*, and *Chiyoda*. This was later called the Battle of Cape Engano, and marks the end of the series of titanic battles which, collectively, are known as the Battle of Leyte Gulf. In terms of tonnage and numbers of ships involved it was the greatest sea battle in history, and achieved the virtual extinction of the Imperial Japanese navy. The Japanese had come close to victory, although more as a result of U.S. mistakes than their own skill. Had the U.S. commanders made use of the intelligence at their disposal, the Center Force would have been stopped sooner and the Northern Force would have been dealt with as well.

THE U.S. FORCES INVADE LEYTE

In July 1944 the USA had the difficult problem to face of what to do next in the Pacific. General Douglas MacArthur favored an assault on the Philippine Islands group and thence Japan, while Admiral Nimitz considered that the U.S. forces should now move toward an invasion of Formosa or of a Japanese-held part of China before the final assault on the Japanese home islands. President Franklin D. Roosevelt had to decide between the two options, whose protagonists argued their cases at a conference held at Pearl Harbor in July. Roosevelt finally came down on the side of MacArthur, and Nimitz, despite having lost the argument, committed his planning staffs wholeheartedly to the task of coordinating army and navy plans for the Philippines operation: MacArthur's forces would take Mindanao, the southernmost large island of the Philippines group, while Nimitz's forces took Yap Island in the Caroline Islands group as an advanced base. The two forces would then combine for the assault on Leyte, and finally as MacArthur went on to take Luzon, the main island of the Philippines, Nimitz would take Iwo Jima and Okinawa, farther to the north, as the bases for the final landings on Japan itself.

First of all the two commanders set about securing themselves adequate forward bases. On September 15 men of the U.S. Amy landed on Morotai Island, in the northern part of the Halmahera Islands group in the Moluccas, secured the island against scant Japanese opposition and set about building an airfield. On the same day U.S. Marines of Major-General Roy S. Geiger's III Amphibious Corps landed on Peleliu, where they encountered resistance as determined as any met by the U.S. forces in World War II. The defense of Peleliu, under the capable leadership of Colonel Kunio Nakagawa, meant that the island was secured by the Americans only on October 13, after each side had suffered heavy losses. The last vestiges of the fighting finally ended on November 25, by which time the army's 85th Division had been brought in to reinforce Major-General W.H. Rupertus's 1st Marine Division. Meanwhile, army troops of Geiger's immediate superior, Vice-Admiral Theodore Wilkinson, of the III Amphibious Corps, had taken Angaur, at the extreme southern tip of the Palau Islands group, during September 17–20, and the vast atoll of Ulithi, some 100 miles (160km) to the west of Yap. The last was

taken without opposition, and soon became the U.S. 3rd Fleet's main base.

To support the Morotai and Peleliu operations by diverting the attention of the Japanese, the aircraft carriers of Admiral Halsey's 3rd Fleet had struck at targets in the Palaus, Ulithi and Yap on September 6, but had met with little opposition. Halsey then moved north against targets in the Philippines during September 9–13. Yet again there was minimal opposition, so Halsey informed Nimitz that the landings planned for Yap and Mindanao were unnecessary, and that the target date for Leyte should be brought forward. The Joint Chiefs of Staff Committee agreed, and with Nimitz's offer of the loan of the III Amphibious and XXIV Corps, MacArthur was able to bring forward the Leyte operation from December 20 to October 20.

The landings on Leyte were preceded by the usual naval operations to suppress Japanese air power. During October 7–16 Halsey's warplanes had struck at Okinawa's airfields before turning to do the same at Formosa. Here, however, two of his cruisers were damaged, and Halsey took the considerable gamble of using them as a decoy for the Japanese air forces, which rose to the bait and were decimated by Halsey's aircraft. These fast carrier sweeps cost Japan some 650 aircraft and their irreplaceable aircrew. Just as significantly, most of the warplanes had been the replacements for those lost in the Battle of the Philippine Sea, sent to Formosa from Japan by Admiral Soemu Toyoda, commander-in-chief of the Combined Fleet. Japan's carriers were now almost naked of aircraft. Halsey's success off Formosa was complemented by the success of three formations of the U.S. Army Air Forces, namely the 5th AAF from New Guinea, the 7th AAF from the Marianas and the XX Bomber Command from China, all of which launched major raids at Japanese targets within their ranges.

All was now ready for the Leyte

ABOVE: *U.S. solders display captured Japanese flags.*

invasion by Lieutenant-General Walter Krueger's 6th Army. During October 14–19, the 700 ships of Vice-Admiral Thomas C. Kinkaid's 7th Fleet moved Krueger's 200,000 men from their advanced bases toward Leyte. The two attack forces, the VII Amphibious Force under Rear-Admiral Daniel E. Barbey, and the III Amphibious Force under Vice-Admiral Theodore S. Wilkinson, were supported by the six battleships of Rear-Admiral Jesse B. Oldendorf, which were able to lay down a formidable volume of heavy gunfire to aid the land forces, and by the aircraft operating from the 16 escort carriers of Rear-Admiral Thomas L. Sprague's Task Group 77.4. Providing long-range support and protection were the eight fleet carriers, eight light carriers and six battleships of Halsey's 3rd Fleet. As usual, all of these naval forces were provided with ample cruiser and destroyer support. The one blemish in the otherwise excellent organization for the Leyte operation was a measure of divided command, MacArthur controlling the 6th Army and 7th Fleet, and Halsey the 3rd Fleet. Still smarting from their failure to sink all the Japanese carriers involved in the Battle of the Philippine Sea, the men of the 3rd Fleet had the primary function of seeking out and destroying the Japanese fleet should the occasion arise, the secondary function being the covering of the Leyte operation. This was to have nearly disastrous consequences in the Battle of Leyte Gulf.

To defend the Philippine Islands group, General Tomoyuki Yamashita had the 14th Area Army of 350,000 men. But to cover the possible landing areas and to keep the active Filipino guerrilla movement in check meant that these troops had to be spread over a wide area. On Leyte there was only the 16th Division, commanded by Lieutenant-General Shiro Makino, totaling only 16,000 men. This was part of Lieutenant-General Sosaku Suzuki's 35th Army, entrusted with the defense of the southern Philippines.

The landings took place on October 20 against minimal opposition. The 1st Cavalry and 24th Divisions of Major-General Franklin C. Sibert's X Corps landed in the area just to the south of Tacloban on the eastern side of the island, and the 96th and 7th Divisions of Major-General John Hodge's XXIV Corps slightly farther south, in the area of Dulag. By midnight on the first day, 132,500 men and nearly 200,000 tons of supplies had been landed. The Americans quickly pressed on inland before the Japanese could strengthen their defenses. Part of the 16th Division had established a beach-head on each side of the Juanico Strait, between Samar and Leyte, by October 24. By October 30, the U.S. forces occupied most of the north-eastern corner of the island, as far west as Carigara on the north coast, and in the west as far as the lower slopes of the central mountain chain as far south as Burauen, although the front line was only lightly held. MacArthur, and President Sergio Osmena of the Philippines, came ashore on October 22.

By November 30 the Americans had pushed further forward, but Suzuki had moved into Leyte. As the 16th Division fought stubbornly to delay the U.S. forces, Suzuki would ship in another 45,000 men and 10,000 tons of supplies before December 11, when all Japanese ship movements to Leyte were halted. Progress into the mountains was virtually halted, and heavy rain made movement extraordinarily difficult. The X Corps edged slowly toward Limon and Pinamopoan, on the north coast, by means of land and amphibious advances, and by November 7 the XXIV Corps tried unsuccessfully to take the mountains overlooking the main Japanese base of Ormoc, on the west coast, against superb defense by the 16th and 26th Divisions. The Japanese defense was finally outflanked on December 7 when the U.S. 77th Division was landed just south of Ormoc. Limon and Ormoc both fell on December 10, and forces from north and south met at Libungao on December 20. The Japanese were now cut off from their one remaining port, Palompon, to which a few sailing vessels were still operating. Organized Japanese resistance ended on December 25, but mopping-up operations against the starving Japanese continued for some time. A beach-head on Samar had already been secured, and on December 15 a U.S. brigade landed on the island of Mindoro to start building an airfield for the forthcoming Luzon operations. By the beginning of 1945 the Americans had secured Leyte, the southern tip of Samar, and enclaves on the south and west coasts of Mindoro. Japanese losses up to this time exceeded 70,000, those of the Americans being 15,584.

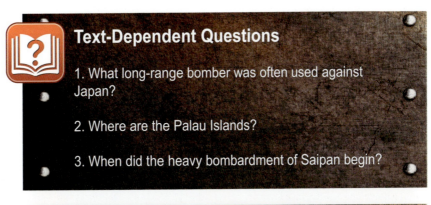

Text-Dependent Questions

1. What long-range bomber was often used against Japan?

2. Where are the Palau Islands?

3. When did the heavy bombardment of Saipan begin?

Research Projects

Summarize the events of the Philippines Campaign.

WORLD WAR II

Chapter Four
THE BATTLES OF KOHIMA AND IMPHAL

Lieutenant-General Renya Mutaguchi's Japanese 15th Army crossed the Chindwin river early in March 1944, with every man carrying enough ammunition and food for three weeks, a supply train of 3,000 horses and 5,000 oxen, and 17 mountain guns carried on 10 elephants. The Japanese objective was Imphal, the great logistical base the British were creating for the liberation of Burma. With enemies on three sides building, the Japanese leadership in Burma now believed that a passive posture was too dangerous. The best course, and one suited to the Japanese temperament, was to knock out the nearest opponents. It was a huge gamble, because there were no roads or bridges between Burma and Assam, and victory had to be won while the supplies lasted. The Japanese, however, had spotted the weakness in the widely dispersed British positions. Although Mutaguchi had only three divisions, he was able to choose the points to strike. In February a limited offensive in the Arakan had drawn the reserves of Lieutenant-General William J. Slim's 14th Army to that area. Mutaguchi believed it would be a month at least before the 14th Army could be reinforced in Assam. He was to be proved wrong: the British flew in reinforcements and supplies in days, but Mutaguchi's utter defeat resulted not only from the Allies' superior air power, armor, and artillery, but also from the capacity of the British, Indian and Gurkha infantry, over a period of four months, to take on and defeat the Japanese in close combat, which had hitherto been a particular speciality of the Japanese.

The Battle of Imphal is, of course, simply a label for a whole series of battles fought from March 15 to June 22.

Hitherto the Japanese had seemed invincible, but the retraining of the British and Indian troops had not merely improved tactics and weapon skills, but had also unleashed courage and devotion fully equal to coping with the Japanese. The medical services had also greatly reduced losses from tropical diseases.

When the battle began the British had drawn back from 20 to 50 miles (32–80km) from the Chindwin river, watching the barrier with army patrols and an observation corps of tribesmen (called V Force), organized by British officers. The closest point of the railway from India to Jorhat in the far north-east was Dimapur, and from here the only supply route was the road through Kohima, a small settlement on a ridge providing a natural defensive position, to Imphal, a valley about 15 miles (24km) wide, overlooked by mountains rising to 6,900ft (2100m). Here the roads from Kohima, Sangshak, Tamu, and Tiddim met, as well as a smaller road from Bishenpur to Silchar which also gave access to Imphal. Road in the context of this area is a purely nominal term, for these surfaces were unmetaled and only just motorable until the military engineers improved them. Troops moving by road could be blocked or ambushed, while movement through the jungle up and down the dense forest on the mountain slopes was painfully slow.

Imphal was therefore a strategic centre of communications. Three airfields, two of them capable of all-weather operations, had been constructed, and the area included dumps of supplies and ammunition of all kinds, the headquarters of the IV Corps, commanded by Lieutenant-General G.A.P. Scoones, and a garrison for the Indian 23rd Division. Two other

OPPOSITE: A man of the British 14th Army reports the results of a reconnaissance effort in Burma during 1944.

RIGHT: The wreckage of the district commissioner's bungalow, scene of some of the most savage fighting in the Battle of Kohima, itself one of the bitterest fights of World War II.

formations were also in the area, the Indian 17th Division around Tiddim and the Indian 20th Division around Tamu. The 2nd Division, which reinforced Kohima, was British. Because of the width of the front and the nature of the country, the three Indian divisions were each spread over some 40–50 miles

(65–80km). Imphal is 130 miles (210km) from Dimapur and 90 miles (145km) from Kohima, and the 17th Division was 160 miles (255km) south and the 20th Division 80 miles (130km) to the south-east. There was nothing except V Force and a battalion of the Assam Rifles between Homalin, where the right-flank

launch a full-scale offensive, plans had to be made to form a solid defensive ring round Imphal. This meant pulling in the outlying units, but not too fast: they had to delay the Japanese in order to allow the mass of civilian labor, working on the roads and in the depots, to be removed to safety, but they were not to tangle with the Japanese too closely and become pinned down.

The real danger was in the north, or the British left. The great weakness of the IV Corps' position was that its supply lines did not come from rear to front but along the front from left to right. If the Japanese were to take or bypass Kohima, cutting the railroad at Dimapur, not only the IV Corps but also Lieutenant-General Joseph W. Stilwell's Chinese divisions would be starved to death. British intelligence suggested that the biggest force that could come by this roadless northern route was a regiment. In fact a nasty shock was in store: the whole of the Japanese 31st Division arrived at Kohima, cutting the road between there and Dimapur.

The Japanese tactics, which so far had proved successful against the British, were simple and effective: they would encircle the opposition, establishing road blocks of bunkers behind, the brigades thus trapped being either caught between two fires, or being forced to leave the road in panic, seeking to escape through the jungle, abandoning all their guns, equipment and vehicles in the process. The Japanese now discovered, however, that this was no longer the pattern of events. The 14th Army had a new spirit. If cut off, its units and formations stood to fight until they had prevailed or were relieved, and if they could not be supplied by road they were nourished from the air. All the logistics units had been taught to do the same. This the Japanese had yet to find out, although they could have taken warning from the beating they had taken in Arakan in February.

The Japanese, accordingly, spread their effort: their 33rd Division against the 17th Division, 15th Division against the 23rd Division, two separate columns from the 33rd and 15th Divisions reaching for the 20th Division, and the 31st Division against Kohima.

division of the Japanese was to cross the Chindwin, and Kohima, where Colonel H.V. Richards had been sent to organize the defense with such details as could be gleaned from reinforcement camps and logistic units. The initial dispositions of the IV Corps were, in any case, for an advance, not a defense. They were very vulnerable to an aggressive foe, such as the Japanese, who had the initiative and could strike wherever they chose. When the excellent British intelligence system began in February and March to receive evidence that the Japanese were about to

At first the situation as seen by Slim looked very dangerous. Elements of all three of his divisions were cut off and had to fight their way out with some loss, while a Japanese force appeared in the heart of the Imphal base and seized the commanding height of Nunshigum. The Kohima garrison was cut off, and the Japanese then blocked the road behind the relieving brigade. Once again it seemed that the Japanese would succeed in routing their opponents. Stilwell, who

OPPOSITE: A Gurkha soldier moves up toward a Japanese position. Throughout World War II, the Gurkhas showed themselves to be magnificent fighting men, especially in close combat.

BELOW: British troops in the wreckage of Kohima after the Japanese had been driven back.

had a very low opinion of "limeys" and their fighting ability, was very alarmed: halting his own operation, he offered Slim a Chinese division to protect Dimapur and the railroad, on which he and his large engineer force, building the road, entirely depended. Slim, however, and his chiefs, General Sir Henry Giffard and Admiral Lord Louis Mountbatten, were steadfast. Stilwell's offer was politely refused and he was told to get on with his own operation. To the surprise of the Japanese the Indian 5th Division, which had been drawn into the Arakan fighting as they had planned and should have been a month's journey away, was flown in complete with its artillery to Imphal. The 5th Division won the Battle of Nunshigum. The Indian 50th Parachute Brigade, sent hastily to Sangshak, was cut off but stood and fought until ordered to break out, thus giving Scoones invaluable days to rearrange his

defences. The British 2nd Division was sent to break through to Kohima and open the road to Imphal. The Japanese here made the fatal mistake of fighting tooth and nail for the Kohima ridge: had they bypassed it and made a dash for Dimapur, things might have turned out badly for the British, for a long delay might have starved out the Imphal garrison.

The course of events seemed very slow, as always in jungle warfare, but Scoones was tightening his defenses and fought battle after battle, slowly going over to the offensive. On June 4 Mutaguchi ordered Lieutenant-General Kotoku Sato to pull his 31st Division back from Kohima, and shortly after this his 15th Army collapsed, only fragments of it managing to stagger back across the Chindwin, weakened by starvation and disease, and leaving behind 30,000 dead.

WORLD WAR II

Chapter Five
THE U.S. ARMY CLEARS THE PHILIPPINES

The clearance of the last Japanese resistance on Leyte by the end of 1944 opened the way for the assault on Luzon, the main island of the Philippines group, where General Tomoyuki Yamashita and the majority of the men of his 14th Area Army were located. Yamashita had some 260,000 troops under his command, and these he divided into three main groupings to defend the key areas of the island. Yamashita himself and 152,000 men formed the "Shobo" Group in the north of the island; Lieutenant-General Rikichi Tsukada and 30,000 men formed the "Kembu" Group in the Bataan peninsula area; and Lieutenant-General Shizuo Yokoyama and 80,000 men were the

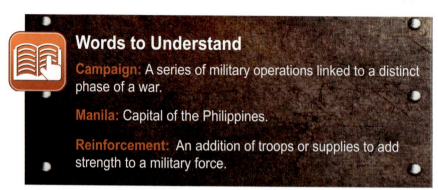

Words to Understand

Campaign: A series of military operations linked to a distinct phase of a war.

Manila: Capital of the Philippines.

Reinforcement: An addition of troops or supplies to add strength to a military force.

"Shimbu Group," entrusted with the task of holding the rest of the island, including **Manila**, the capital. Yamashita appreciated that once the Americans had

landed he could expect no **reinforcements** and therefore decided on a slow defensive campaign, the intention being to tie down as many U.S. troops as possible for

as long as possible. With only 150 operational aircraft he could not hope to contest mastery of the air, even at the outset of the **campaign**, therefore *kamikaze* suicide aircraft were to be used against the U.S. invasion fleet approaching the landing areas, thus giving the pilots as many targets as possible. The U.S. forces would be allowed to land without opposition, as Yamashita thought it unwise to risk his forces in the presence of overwhelming U.S air and naval gunfire support, and the Japanese would pull back slowly to the inaccessible mountains, where strong defensive positions had been prepared so that the Japanese soldiers could sell their lives as expensively as possible. The Japanese commander had no intention of being drawn into a costly street battle for Manila, and on the whole his plans were sound.

The U.S. plan was also simple. Lieutenant General Walter C. Krueger's 6th Army had some 200,000 men, and was to be convoyed from Leyte to Lingayen Gulf, 100 miles (160km) north of Manila, on the west coast, by the 850 vessels of Vice-Admiral Kinkaid's 7th Fleet. As at Leyte, Vice-Admiral Oldendorf's battleship force was to provide heavy gunfire support, while long-range cover and air support would come from the aircraft carriers of Admiral Halsey's 3rd Fleet and from the airfields on Leyte, now occupied by the aircraft of General George C. Kenney's Far East Air Forces. After landing, the 6th Army would advance south across the central plain of Luzon to Manila and its magnificent harbor. Other forces would spread out to engage the Japanese wherever they could be found.

The invasion fleet left Leyte Gulf on January 2, 1945 for Lingayen Gulf, where the landings were to take place on January 9. Although the *kamikaze* aircraft did not achieve the results for

OPPOSITE: *Men of the U.S. Army's 40th Infantry Division in action on Panay Island in the Philippines group. Only part of the division was used, this landing on the south coast at Iloilo on March 18, 1945.*

Men of the U.S. 6th Army start to land at Lingayen Gulf on Luzon, the main island of the Philippines group, on January 9, 1945. At first the Americans met only limited resistance as the Japanese commander, General Tomoyuki Yamashita, wished to preserve as much as possible of his 14th Army for a protracted defense.

which the Japanese had hoped, many warships were severely damaged and the escort carrier *Ommaney Bay* was so badly damaged that she had to be abandoned. On January 7, however, the Americans launched a series of major raids against Japanese airfields on Luzon, and the Japanese aircraft which escaped destruction were flown to Formosa. It was a sad tactical error on the part of the Japanese, the main damage by the *kamikaze* aircraft having been done to warships rather than the more vulnerable and important troop transports.

On January 9 the 6th Army started to pour ashore at Lingayen: on the left was Major-General Innis P. Swift's I Corps of the 6th and 43rd Divisions, and on the right Major-General Oscar W. Griswold's XIV Corps of the 37th and 40th Divisions. By nightfall, the 68,000 men of the two corps were well placed in a beach-head 17 miles (27km) wide and 4 miles (6.5km) deep. The XIV Corps was to advance to Manila, while the I Corps on the left flank dealt with any Japanese interference from the Shobo Group. Swift's corps found the Japanese prepared positions very tough, and Griswold was unwilling to advance very

far until the I Corps had cleared his left flank. But by January 23, the XIV Corps was in the area of Clark Field, where it was involved in a week of heavy fighting before it could move on yet again.

Lieutenant-General Robert L. Eichelberger's 8th Army had assumed responsibility for the southern islands of the Philippine archipelago when the 6th Army sailed north for the Luzon campaign, but it was now decided to use this to help Krueger's formation. On January 30, therefore, Major-General Charles P. Hall's XI Corps landed in the Subic Bay area, seizing Olongapo before moving off east to Danilupihan, which fell on February 5, completing the isolation of the Kembu Group in the Bataan peninsula. Yamashita had foreseen this possibility, however, and refused to have major forces locked up in the peninsula as had been the case with the Americans in 1942. So before the pincers of XIV and XI Corps closed at Danilupihan most of the Kembu Group had reached temporary safety to the north-east. Even so, the XI Corps had two weeks of costly fighting before it, clearing the remnants of the Japanese group from Bataan on February 21.

The other 8th Army formation used on Luzon was the 11th Airborne Division, commanded by Major-General Joseph M. Swing. On January 31, two regiments of the division were landed at Nasugbu, south of Manila, moving quickly inland. The third regiment was dropped on Tagaytay Ridge farther inland, on February 3, encountering only small-scale resistance before linking with the rest of the division, which then moved north toward Manila, which was reached on the following day.

Although ordered by Yamashita not to defend the city, Rear-Admiral Mitsuji Iwafuchi and 18,000 fanatical naval troops decided to make a last stand. The 37th Division drove down from the north into the city, while the 1st Cavalry Division moved around the east of Manila to link up with the 11th Airborne Division. Casualties on both sides were appalling, and by February 22 the Japanese had been driven back into the old walled town, where they made their last stand. Manila was almost totally

destroyed in the fighting, the Japanese having fired great sections of streets as a defensive measure. By the end of the battle on March 4, some 100,000 Filipino civilians, at least 16,665 Japanese, and 1,000 Americans had been killed, with another 5,500 Americans wounded. Manila was only half the prize, however, for the harbour in Manila Bay could not be used until the Japanese garrisons on Corregidor and Fort Drum had been eliminated. An amphibious assault and airborne landing on Corregidor, on

February 16, were followed by severe hand-to-hand fighting before the island was declared secure on February 27. Some 4,417 Japanese dead were found, and only 19 prisoners were taken. U.S. losses were 209 killed and 725 wounded. Fort Drum fell quickly on April 13, after fuel oil and petrol had been poured into its ventilators and set on fire, incinerating the entire Japanese garrison. A landing was made on Caballo Island during the same day, but did not fall for two weeks, whereas Carabao Island fell without a fight.

By the middle of May the southern half of Luzon had been cleared, but Yamashita was still fighting an excellent campaign in the mountains of the north. For the rest of the war the Americans tried in every way they could to flush the Japanese out, but in the end were content to keep them bottled up in the Cordillera Central and Sierra Madre. When he surrendered at the end of the war, Yamashita still had 50,000 disciplined men. Yet the Luzon campaign had cost the Japanese 192,000 dead and just under 10,000 captured in combat, compared with fewer than 8,000 U.S. dead and 33,000 wounded.

As the 6th Army was reducing Luzon, the 8th Army was involved in clearing the southern Philippines, defended by the remaining 100,000 men of Lieutenant-General Sosaku Suzuki's 35th Army. Between February and August the 8th Army was involved in some 50 amphibious landings. Normally

OPPOSITE: General Tomoyuki Yamashita surrenders the remnants of his 14th Army on September 2, 1945, after the end of World War II. The surrender was taken by two ex-prisoners of war, Lieutenant-General Jonathan Wainwright, who had surrendered the last U.S. forces in the Philippines on May 6, 1942, and Lieutenant-General A.E. Percival, who had surrendered the British and commonwealth forces in Singapore on February 25, 1942.

ABOVE: Men of the 5th Marine Division are pinned down on the black volcanic sand of Red Beach, at the southern end of the U.S. landing on Iwo Jima on 19 February, 1945.

the pattern was similar: the U.S. forces landed and the Japanese pulled back into the interior of the island in question, where they were mopped up by local Filipino forces once the U.S. forces had secured their main objectives and pulled out for the next landing. The exception to this rule was Mindanao, where Suzuki had two good divisions. A series of U.S. landings on the north, south and west coasts, with all forces pushing on into the center of the island, led to the 35th Army being cut off, but it nonetheless held out in two major groups in the east of the island for the rest of the war. The 8th Army's campaign had cost 2,556 U.S. dead and 9,412 wounded but, as usual, Japanese losses were much higher, being some 50,000 in all.

THE IWO JIMA AND OKINAWA CAMPAIGNS

The fall of the Philippines sealed the fate of Japan, largely as Japanese shipping could no longer move between the home islands and the rich Southern Resources Area for raw materials and oil. The Americans, however, were still to face

serious problems in their final approach to the Japanese home islands, principally from fanatical Japanese defense on the islands of Iwo Jima and Okinawa. The capture of these was to be one of the three final preparatory phases to the invasion of Japan proper, the other two being the destruction of what was left of Japan's merchant fleet by the U.S. submarine force, and the destruction of Japan's industrial potential by Boeing B-29 Superfortress heavy bombers, operating from China and the Marianas.

Iwo Jima is a small volcanic island 4.67 miles (7.5km) long by 2.5 miles (4km) wide, and of considerable significance despite its miniscule size. Lying at the foot of the Bonin Islands chain, south of the main Japanese island of Honshu, Iwo Jima was a great asset to the side which controlled it: in Japanese hands, aircraft were able to operate from its two airfields to attack Boeing B-29 Superfortress heavy bombers, operating from the Mariana Islands group against Japan, and in U.S. hands the airfields could be used as emergency landing fields for crippled bombers, and also as bases

for long-range escort fighters to protect the bombers over Japan itself. At this time the Japanese were also building a third airfield.

Fully conscious of the island's importance, the Japanese were determined to prevent Iwo Jima from falling into U.S. hands. Lieutenant-General Tadamichi Kuribayashi had under his command some 22,000 men from army and navy combat units. For months these men had been honeycombing the northern plateau with strongpoints, gun emplacements and other bomb- and gunfire-proof positions. Kuribayashi realized this type of defense would limit him to static operations, but saw that there could be no alternative in so small an area and in the face of overwhelming U.S. matériel superiority.

The U.S. assault was preceded by the most intense softening process yet seen in the Pacific war, with more than two months of incessant bombing, followed before the landings by a continuous three-day barrage by six battleships and their supporting forces. Under the overall command of Admiral Nimitz in

Hawaii, the assault force was under the local command of Admiral Spruance's 5th Fleet: the 3rd and 5th Fleets were in fact the same ships, the former designation used when Admiral Halsey commanded and the latter when they were led by Spruance. The land force commander was Lieutenant-General Holland M. Smith, the assault force itself being Lieutenant-General Harry Schmidt's V Amphibious Corps of three U.S .Marine divisions.

The landings were made on February 19, 1945, and were met with determined and accurate Japanese fire as the vast pre-landing bombardment had, inevitably, failed to crush the Japanese defences. The landing area was a black volcanic sand beach on the south-eastern side of the island, the landing forces being Major-General Keller E. Rockey's 5th Marine Division on the left and Major-General Clifton B. Cates's 4th Marine Division on the right, with Major-General Graves B. Erskine's 3rd Marine Division remaining at sea as a floating reserve. Despite some 2,420 casualties, the marines made good

progress, cutting the island in two by the end of the first day. The next day, part of the 5th Marine Division turned south to assault the dominating heights of Mount Suribachi, at the southern tip of the island. As usual, the Japanese defense was unflinching, and it was not until the morning of February 23 that the U.S. flag was hoisted on the summit of the volcano.

The 4th Marine Division, meanwhile, was making slow progress toward the north, fighting every inch of the way through the elaborate and well concealed Japanese defenses. Elements of the 3rd Marine Division came ashore to aid the 4th Marine Division on February 21, with the rest of the division landing two days later. Thereafter, all three divisions of V Amphibious Corps began to creep forward a few hundred yards every day, the 5th Division on the left, the 3rd in the center, and the 4th on the right, supported the whole way by the guns and aircraft of the 5th Fleet. Vastly superior U.S. strength had its effect, and the Japanese were driven steadily north before the marines. By March 11 Kuribayashi's last survivors had been penned up in an area around Kitano Point, Iwo Jima's northernmost extremity. But it was only on March 16 that the island was declared secure, and on March 26 that the last Japanese resistance ceased.

The Marine losses were 6,891 dead and 18,070 wounded; of the Japanese, almost the entire garrison, as a mere 212 prisoners, was taken. Yet the value of the island was proved when 16 crippled B-29s landed safely on the island. By the end of the war, it has been estimated, the lives of 24,761 aircrew had been saved, 2,251

ABOVE: *A U.S. marine wastes as little time as possible as he operates in the "Death Valley" area of Iwo Jima.*

OPPOSITE: *The U.S. forces which landed in Okinawa on April 1, 1945 were two corps, one comprising two U.S. Army divisions and the other two U.S. Marine Corps divisions. These are U.S. marines, who were involved in some notably savage combat in the area.*

B-29s having been able to land on the island in emergencies.

The final stage of the advance toward Japan was to be the conquest of the Ryukyu group, a tail of islands stretching south from Japan itself. Okinawa is the largest island in the chain, some 60 miles (95km) long and between 2 and 18.5 miles (3 and 30km) wide, with a considerably varied terrain. Virtually unknown outside Japan before the war, Okinawa was a difficult problem for the U.S. planners, about which reconnaissance aircraft had been unable to secure good information. It was estimated that the garrison numbered about 65,000 men, with the main defensive area likely to be in the southern third of the island, where its four airfields were located. In fact, Okinawa was garrisoned by the 130,000 men of Lieutenant-General Mitsuru Ushijima's 32nd Army, and there were also 450,000 civilians on the island. Ushijima had been ordered to hold the island at all

costs: it was expected by the Japanese high command that *kamikaze* attacks on the U.S. fleet during the landing would be decisive, the losses in ships being sufficient to force the Americans to withdraw, enabling the 32nd Army to mop up any forces that had landed. Ushijima elected to fight the same sort of campaign as Yamashita in Luzon: he would attempt to hold the strategically important southern end of the island from a great complex of fortifications built into the hills, thus compelling the U.S. forces to mount a costly series of frontal assaults in order to break through his defenses. Despite the hopes of the high command, Ushijima had no illusions of being able to hold the Americans on the beaches should the *kamikaze* attacks fail.

As at Iwo Jima, the responsibility of getting the troops to Okinawa and protecting them once they had landed was allocated to Spruance's 5th Fleet, with the Joint Expeditionary Force led by

Vice-Admiral Richmond K. Turner. The land operations were to be the job of Lieutenant-General Simon Bolivar Buckner's 10th Army of 180,000 men, with ample reserves held in New Caledonia and other islands farther to the north of this southern base. The beach area selected for the landings was just to the north of Hagushi Bay, on the western side of the island. Two corps were to land in the first wave: the 6th and 1st Marine Divisions of Major-General Roy S. Geiger's III Amphibious Corps on the left, and the 7th and 96th Divisions of Major-General John B. Hodge's XIV Corps on the right. As the island was beyond the range of U.S. land-based tactical air support, the 10th Army and the invasion fleet would be wholly reliant on the carrierborne warplanes of Vice-Admiral Marc A. Mitscher's Fast Carrier Task Force (Task Force 58) and the four British carriers of Vice-Admiral Sir Bernard Rawling's Task Force 57. Unfortunately for the Americans,

Okinawa lay within range of Japanese aircraft from Formosa and Japan.

Scheduled for April 1, the main landings would be preceded by the usual intense bombardment and the capture of a number of subsidiary targets in the area as forward bases. On March 26, the 77th Division, under Major-General Andrew D. Bruce, was landed in the Kerama Islands group, some 20 miles (32km) south-west of the main beaches on Okinawa, to secure them as a fleet anchorage. Little resistance was met, and the capture of a large number of suicide boats was enough to ease the minds of the naval command. On March 31, the 77th Division moved forward to capture the Keise Islands group, only 10 miles (16km) from the main assault area, as a heavy artillery base for the support of the III and XIV Corps. During the same period, the carrier forces ranged over the area trying to neutralize the Japanese *kamikaze* aircraft, of which some 193 had been dispatched, the U.S. and British destroying 169 of them. Those that got through, however, inflicted heavy losses on the U.S. carriers, which were lacking the armored flight decks of the British vessels. Nonetheless, the carrier activities had destroyed part of

Japan's *kamikaze* potential that might otherwise have been used against the more vulnerable invasion fleet.

The vessels carrying the invasion force, some 300 warships and 1,139 other ships, had meanwhile approached Okinawa, and the four assault divisions went ashore without opposition on April 1, securing a good beach-head for the 60,000 men who landed on the first day. A feint attack by the 2nd Marine Division against the south-east coast helped to distract the attention of the 32nd Army as the main force landed. The next day the two corps set about their allotted tasks. The III Amphibious Corps turned left, where it encountered little resistance in securing the northern two-thirds of the island by April 13. This was a reversal of Buckner's earlier decision to leave the clearance of the north until after the main Japanese positions in the south had been overrun. The last organized resistance in the north was finally overcome 20 April 20 on the Motobu peninsula, although many Japanese escaped into the hills to wage a guerrilla campaign against the Americans. While the 6th Marine Division undertook this task, Buckner had also changed his mind regarding another earlier decision, and now

ordered the 77th Division to take the island of Ie Shima, where there were 2,000 Japanese troops and a labour force, so that airstrips could be built for tactical support warplanes. The division landed on 16 April, securing the western half by the end of the day. But it was to be a bloody eight days before the rest of the island could be overrun.

Back in the south, the XIV Corps had been having a far rougher experience. After pushing through to the east coast, across from the landing areas on the west coast by 3 April, the corps had turned right as the III Amphibious Corps turned left. As yet little opposition had been met, but the few prisoners taken revealed the reason for this: the 32nd Army was waiting in the south, and the real battle had yet to begin. On 4 April, XIV Corps reached the Machinato Line, the US divisions pressing on slowly against strengthening resistance before being brought to a halt by 12 April.

Ushijima's plan was proceeding as intended, but the Japanese commander then deviated with costly results. The Japanese 24th and 62nd Divisions launched a two-day counter-offensive, which the US forces repelled with heavy losses. A temporary lull settled over the southern battlefield on 14 April as both sides rested and reassessed the situation. His frontal assaults having failed, Buckner now determined to launch a surprise attack by the 27th Division, previously the army's floating reserve. The attack went in on 19 April and was a failure, as was that of the following day. The Machinato Line was finally pierced on 24 April, but the Americans were again brought to a halt on 28 April, this time in front of the Japanese main defence, the Shuri Line. Buckner paused again to reconsider his approach and rest his weary divisions.

Meanwhile the first *kamikaze* aircraft attacks had been launched on 7 April against the ships lying off the island, and although 383 of the 355 *kamikaze* and 340 conventional attack aircraft had been shot down, damage had been caused to many ships and quite a few smaller vessels had been sunk. At the same time, the biggest *kamikaze* of them all was approaching the island. This was

the super-battleship *Yamato*, escorted by one light cruiser and eight destroyers. Carrying just enough fuel to get to Okinawa and loaded with as much ammunition as it could carry, the *Yamato* was to sink as many U.S. ships as possible before sinking in shallow water to serve as a maritime fortress. Encountered by Mitscher's carrierborne warplanes on the afternoon of 7 April, the *Yamato* survived four hours of attack before sinking, together with the cruiser and four destroyers. The aerial *kamikaze* effort was then resumed, with more than 3,000 missions launched on 12–13 April. The U.S. losses were heavy, with 21 ships sunk, 43 very seriously damaged, and 23 badly damaged.

Ushijima launched an offensive by the 24th Division on 3 May, but this had been bloodily repulsed by the next day. Buckner, meanwhile, was reorganizing his forces for the final offensive. For Buckner's attack of 11 May, the III Corps moved into the right of the line with the XIV Corps moving into the left, which pierced the Japanese defences at both ends of the line. Ushijima began to pull back from the Shuri Line on 21 May, and by the end of the month the Americans had broken through toward the south coast. However, there was still plenty of fight left in the 32nd Army, and the hills of the southern tip of Okinawa suited their tactics admirably. Buckner pressed home his offensive against gallant resistance, and the last organized defence ended on 22 June. Ushijima committed suicide just before the end, with Buckner having died from wounds received from artillery fire four days earlier. The fighting continued

OPPOSITE: *Fitted with the turret of the M8 self-propelled gun, with its 2.95-inch (75-mm) short-barrel howitzer, and carrying sand bags for additional protection along the tops of their hulls, these LVT(A)4 amtraks are heading for the assault beaches on Okinawa.*

ABOVE: *Soldiers of the U.S. Marine Corps and the "stars and stripes" on top of Mount Suribachi, the highest point of Iwo Jima, on February 23, 1945.*

sporadically for another few days, and Okinawa was declared secure on 2 July.

The cost to both sides had been very high: the US forces lost 7,373 men killed and 32,056 wounded on land, and 5,000 killed and 4,600 wounded at sea; the Japanese losses were 107,500 dead and 7,400 taken prisoner, with possibly another 20,000 dead in their bunkers as a result of the US tactics of using flame-throwers and burning petrol, and then sealing the bunkers with demolition charges. In matériel terms, the USA had lost 36 ships sunk and 368 damaged, as well as 763 aircraft, and Japan 16 ships sunk and at least 4,000 aircraft expended.

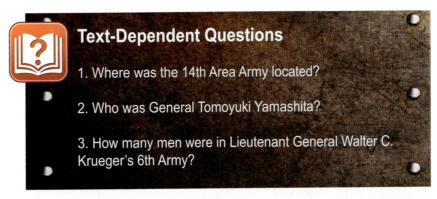

Text-Dependent Questions

1. Where was the 14th Area Army located?

2. Who was General Tomoyuki Yamashita?

3. How many men were in Lieutenant General Walter C. Krueger's 6th Army?

Research Projects

Summarize the events of Japan's occupation of the Philippines between 1942 and 1945.

WORLD WAR II

Chapter Six
THE STRATEGIC BOMBER WAR AGAINST JAPAN

The Americans and the British placed great faith in strategic bombing during World War II, partly because it offered the chance for costly land operations to be avoided or made less costly by the reduction of the opponent's ability to fight, and was also, at least during the early stages of the war, the only practical means of striking back at Germany and Japan. Once the campaigns had got under way they generated their own momentum and thus became almost impossible to stop, even in the event of the Allied leaders wishing to flout public and military opinion.

In the war against Japan, the bombing campaign was exclusively a U.S. effort, culminating in the use of the Boeing B-29 Superfortress heavy bomber for day and night pinpoint and area attacks on Japan's vulnerable civilian, industrial, transport, fuel, and communications systems. The campaign began in a very small but significant way on April 18, 1942 when, launched from the deck of the aircraft carrier *Hornet*, some 800 miles (1300km) from Tokyo, 25 North American B-25 Mitchell twin-engined medium bombers of the U.S. Army Air Forces struck at Tokyo and then flew on to China. The raid lacked any military importance, but it was a profound shock to the Japanese people, and came as an important boost to Allied morale at a very black time.

There were no more raids in 1942, and 1943 was devoted mostly to the building of Major-General Claire L. Chennault's 14th Army Air Force in China. This had begun life as the American Volunteer Group, flying fighters for Generalissimo Chiang Kai-shek against the Japanese in China, had become the China Air Task Force after the USA's entry into the war against Japan, and was now in the process of being built up into a powerful offensive and strategic weapon. The efficiency of Chennault's air force is attested by the fact that, in 1944, the Japanese launched a series of very large offensives to deprive him of his airfields. It should be noted, however, that as yet Chennault's bombers had struck only at targets within China, and as far afield as Formosa to the east and Manchuria to the north-east.

In May 1944 the first B-29s arrived in India en route to China, and from the latter's bases these were at last able to strike at targets in southern Japan. The headquarters for this new and rapidly growing strategic force was the XX Bomber Command. The first B-29 raid was made on June 5, the objective being railway communications in the Bangkok region of Thailand. Further exploratory missions followed before the B-29s made their first raids on Japan on June 15. Although based on airfields in the Calcutta area of India, the B-29s staged through Chinese airfields, whose runways had been lengthened by means of Chinese labor, and fuel brought in by the thousands of tons. Striking from this forward base area, the B-29s raided

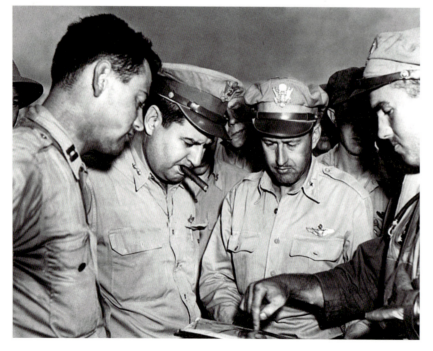

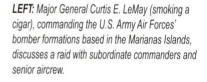

LEFT: *Major General Curtis E. LeMay (smoking a cigar), commanding the U.S. Army Air Forces' bomber formations based in the Marianas Islands, discusses a raid with subordinate commanders and senior aircrew.*

OPPOSITE: *The heavy bomber type which blasted and burned the heart out of Japan in 1944–45 was the Boeing B-29 Superfortress. This was flown by an 11-man crew in the form of a pilot, co-pilot, flight engineer, bombardier, navigator, radio operator, radar observer, two blister gunners, a dorsal gunner, and a tail gunner.*

Japanese steel production in Kyushu, the island at the south-west end of the chain of Japanese home islands.

Commanded by Major-General Curtis E. LeMay, the XX Bomber Command went from strength to strength between June and December 1944. The main trouble lay in the fact that there was still no adequate land route to China, which meant the B-29s had to remain based in India, too far from Japan for raids to be directly launched. The bombers still had to stage through China, refueling from aircraft which arrived with fuel instead of bombs. Even from China, the B-29s were able to range only as far as Kyushu, where they met with determined Japanese fighter

opposition. Armed with 12 0.5-inch (12.7-mm) machine guns and one 20-mm cannon, however, the B-29s were able to give a good account of themselves. Well streamlined and fitted with four powerful engines, they were also very fast, giving the Japanese fighters little time to get into the attack, their own speed superiority being marginal.

The main weight of the strategic bombing campaign was not to come from China but rather from the Marianas, the final objective of Admiral Nimitz's Central Pacific offensive. As soon as Saipan, Guam and Tinian had been captured in July and August 1944, Boeing B-17 and Consolidated B-24 bombers of the army air forces moved

onto the captured airfields, their objectives being not targets in Japan, but in Iwo Jima and the Bonin Islands farther to the north, in preparation for the landings soon to take place. But while these raids got under way, engineers were hard at work lengthening and strengthening the existing runways, and building a vast complex of bases wherever room could be found. As soon as adequate facilities were ready in October, the first B-29s of the XXI Bomber Command moved in and set about preparing for the assault on Japan.

At first only exploratory missions were undertaken, the B-29s from the Marianas blooding themselves in a raid on Truk on October 28. By November all

was ready, and the B-29s launched their first sorties against Japan on November 24, when more than 100 bombers raided an aircraft production facility on the outskirts of Tokyo. For the rest of the year the B-29s continued to raid Japan, building up a store of experience under combat conditions About four times every three weeks the bombers set off, between 100 and 125 strong. They climbed the whole way, so that when they crossed the Japanese coast they were at altitudes above 30,000 feet (9145m). As with earlier raids from China, fighter opposition was very strong, the Japanese having deployed their best pilots in the most modern aircraft to meet the threat. The fighters over Japan were tough opposition, but the bombers also had to run the gauntlet of other excellent fighters operating from Iwo Jima. The gauntlet naturally had to be run twice, once on the way in and once on the way out. Many bombers, damaged on the way in, were shot down over Japan, while others damaged over Japan were dispatched by the Iwo Jima-based

interceptors on their way back to the Marianas. By the end of 1944, worthwhile results were being achieved, but losses were too high for the campaign to be continued indefinitely. The XXI Bomber Command was losing B-29s at an average of 6 percent per mission, when losses under 5 percent were only acceptable in a prolonged campaign such as this.

In January and February 1945, the Joint Chiefs of Staff Committee met several times in an effort to solve the problems of the strategic campaign against Japan. The results had been quite good, although not as good as had been hoped and expected, but the losses were too high, and the weather at high altitude over Japan was very poor, throwing many bombers miles off course and making optical bomb-aiming a chancy business. Radar bombing was, of course, a possibility, but this did not offer the same degree of accuracy, it being small but vital defense facilities that the XXI Bomber Command was trying to hit. And although production had dropped

as a result of civilian dislocation during the bombing, Japan had profited from the small scale of the first raids to the extent of appreciating the problem and dispersing her armament industry. The

ABOVE: *Superfortress heavy bombers are seen on one of the five great airbase complexes which U.S. engineers created on the islands of Tinian (three), Saipan (one) and Guam (one) in the Marianas. These are aircraft of the 29th Bombardment Group of the XXI Bomber Command's 314th Bombardment Wing, based on North Field, Tinian.*

OPPOSITE ABOVE: *As the capital of the Japanese empire, Tokyo came under heavy attack, largely from incendiaries, and suffered enormous devastation as well as a huge loss of life.*

OPPOSITE BELOW: *The Boeing B-29 Superfortress was too fast and flew too high to be a simple target for Japanese antiaircraft guns and interceptors in daylight operations. The Japanese lacked adequate radar and night-fighters so, in practical terms, the Superfortress was invisible to them at night.*

Joint Chiefs of Staff finally decided that what was needed was a greater concentration of effort, and that the best way of securing this was the transfer of the XX Bomber Command from India to the Mariana Islands, so that the whole of General Nathan Twining's 20th Army Air Force could strike together. Until the move could be effected, General Curtis E. LeMay was moved to command the XXI Bomber Command which, it was felt, could profit from his experience.

The arrival of LeMay led to a complete change of tactics, the high-level attacks with HE bombs by day giving way to low-level runs with incendiaries, carried out at night when the Japanese fighter arm was all but impotent. The new tactics were initiated with a fire raid on Tokyo on February 25, 1945, but it was on the night of March 9–10 that LeMay's tactics really proved themselves. Some 334 B-29s raided Tokyo, flying quite low and dropping 1,667 tons of incendiaries The effect was devastating: a vast firestorm was started, gutting the center of the city, in which 83,000 were killed and 100,000 more injured. Some 51 percent of Tokyo was destroyed in this and four other raids during the next 10 days. The bomb tonnage dropped was 9,365, the B-29s carrying three times the normal load when operating at medium to low altitudes. Only 22 aircraft, or some 1.4 percent of the 1,595 sorties dispatched was lost.

Meanwhile, Iwo Jima had been captured, allowing the B-29s to make emergency landings there. At the same time, the problem of Japanese fighters had been removed and the fighters of the VII Fighter Command installed in their place. Flying Republic P-47 Thunderbolt and North American P-51 Mustang fighters, the VII Fighter Command was now able to escort the bombers right over Japan, further reducing the Japanese fighter arm's ability to tackle them. Daylight raids could now be made once more, and as the Japanese fighters were increasingly being grounded for lack of fuel (the result of the U.S. submarine offensive against Japanese tankers) or shot down by the escort fighters, the

B-29s were able to dispense with most of their defensive armament, the weight thus saved being used for an increase in the bomb load.

The campaign reached its climax between May and August 1945, with the arrival of the XX Bomber Command. The B-29s were able to roam at will over Japan, now that the heart of industrial Japan had been burned out. The largest cities after Tokyo, namely Kobe, Osaka,

Nagoya and Yokohama, were all almost entirely destroyed, the superb U.S. target intelligence work enabling virtually every worthwhile target to be wiped out. HE bombs were dropped in industrial areas to break up the concrete foundations on which machine tools sat, and the B-29s also undertook mining operations offshore. By August 1945, the strategic bombing campaign had brought Japan to its knees.

WORLD WAR II

Chapter Seven
VICTORY IN BURMA

With the end of the campaign for Kohima and Imphal, the Allied high command was able to resume its strategic offensive in **Burma**, which was characteristically of the threefold type. The Americans had only one objective in Burma: to open the road to China in order to supply and **mobilize** the myriad Chinese armies against the Japanese occupying mainland China. The British were motivated by the desire to liberate imperial territory, with one school of thought believing that instead of an

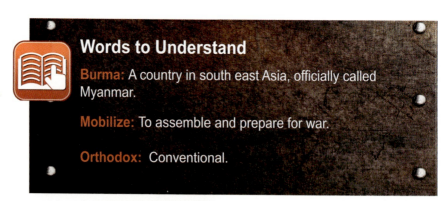

Words to Understand

Burma: A country in south east Asia, officially called Myanmar.

Mobilize: To assemble and prepare for war.

Orthodox: Conventional.

endless campaign in jungle and mountain, an air and seaborne invasion to capture Rangoon would be quicker and cheaper. The third view, strategically very **orthodox**, was held by Lieutenant-General Sir William Slim, commanding the 14th Army. He believed he had the measure of the Japanese, and that if they could only be persuaded to stand and fight in central Burma, the 14th Army could destroy them there. Privately, he resolved to take Rangoon from the landward side, in the belief that this could be done more quickly and reliably than by an amphibious force short of many of the necessary craft and hampered by all the delays imposed by special training and complicated staff planning. This is how the final campaign turned out in Burma in 1945.

The difficulties were formidable. The units of the 14th Army were physically tired, and the 1944 battles and the pursuit through the jungles in the monsoon rain, which had chased the Japanese back across the Chindwin, had resulted in 45,000 casualties, although many of these would recover. The 14th Army would have to advance over the same difficult terrain which had frustrated the Japanese, with a much more modern force making heavy demands on artillery ammunition and petrol. The first calculations of Slim's logistical staff

indicated that no more than 4.5 divisions could be brought to bear because of the difficulties of supply. Yet the Japanese in Burma had admittedly widely deployed, and deficient of modern weapons, some 10.67 divisions and as many as 100,000 service troops had been able to function effectively as infantry on demand. This still formidable force was being rebuilt by the newly appointed commander of the Burma Area Army, Lieutenant-General Hyotaro Kimura.

The 14th Army's logistical difficulties were overcome by enormous feats of engineering and improvisation: hundreds of miles of new roads were built, surfaced with sacking dipped in bitumen; transport ranged from elephants to aircraft; the engineers built rafts, each large enough to float 10 tons of supplies along the rivers, pushed by outboard motors; the greatest Bailey bridge in the world, 1,154 feet (351.75m) long, was built across the Chindwin at Shwegyin; and locomotives to restart the Burmese railroads, wrecked by

OPPOSITE: *Men of the U.S .475th Infantry Regiment in northern Burma during 1944.*

ABOVE: *Men of the Royal Marine commandos in action in Burma during 1945.*

bombing, were flown up in pieces for re-assembly, or were brought up whole on tank transporters all the way over the mountains from India. This effort allowed Slim to deploy six infantry divisions and two tank brigades.

The Japanese, numerous and still determined, fought determinedly until the end, but had been hard hit in 1944. Their diversionary attack in the Arakan in February 1944 had been smashed, and the Chinese Army in India had destroyed the 18th Division by August. The 14th Army had been attacked by 115,000 men and had killed (or caused to die of wounds, sickness, or starvation) 65,000 more. The plan for 1945 was a compromise. In the north the CAI, now commanded by the U.S. Lieutenant-General Dan Sultan, Stilwell having been relieved, with the all-British 36th Division, was to clear northern Burma up to the Chinese border as far as Lashio, while the British XV Corps was to embark on an amphibious campaign among the islands and creeks of the Arakan to pin the Japanese forces there, the 14th Army advancing up to the line of the Irrawaddy river to take Mandalay.

Slim's own plans went a step further than this. His 14th Army had two major formations in the shape of the XXXIII Corps (2nd, 19th, and 20th Divisions

with a brigade of tanks) and the IV Corps (7th and 17th Divisions with a brigade of tanks) plus the 5th Division in reserve. The XXXIII Corps was directed on the Irrawaddy from the north and north-west to cross the river 50 miles (80km) downstream and 100 miles (160km) upstream and close the pincers on Mandalay. This, Slim hoped, would draw the bulk of the Japanese defense to that area. Then, when this was under way, the IV Corps would move with great secrecy down the Gangaw valley, which meant building a completely new first-class road, and with the Royal Air Force holding off every Japanese reconnaissance aeroplane, would thrust for Meiktila. Meiktila and Thazi, on a nodal point of the central road and railway system, comprised the main Japanese supply base, being strategically more important than Mandalay or even Rangoon; if the Japanese armies in central Burma were starved and defeated Rangoon would be indefensible. While the battles of central Burma were at full blast, Slim's staff officers were working on the advance to Rangoon.

All went according to plan, which was implemented, almost alone, by Slim and his 14th Army. However, credit must be given to the contribution of the Chinese 5th and 6th Armies and the 36th

aimed at provoking the Japanese into a counterattack before destroying them.

The XXXIII Corps advanced in the north, the Indian 19th Division crossing the Irrawaddy north of Mandalay in January and turning south along the east bank. The Indian 20th Division crossed 40 miles (65km) farther downstream of the city on February 12 and the British 2nd Division on February 24, on their left. The crossing points were cunningly concealed but were not unopposed. Japanese reaction was prompt, but true to their doctrine they attacked the bridgeheads on a piecemeal basis, which allowed them to be destroyed on the same basis. Then, with all the freedom conferred by air supply and air support, the three divisions fanned out to cut the routes south of Mandalay to Rangoon and east to Maymyo, while inside this envelopment two pincers closed on the city itself. Kimura reacted satisfactorily, by Slim's terms, pulling in his forces for a battle around Mandalay, only to find he had been fooled by an elaborate deception to make him believe that all the weight of the British offensive was in the north. The IV Corps, complete with its armour, had secretly advanced down the Gangaw valley to force a passage across the Irrawaddy some 100 miles (160km) to the south-west of Mandalay and only 50 miles (80km) from the vital depots at Meiktila. Seeing the danger, Kimura switched his forces there, but was too late. By March 1, Major-General D.T. Cowan's Indian 17th Division, with the 255th Tank Brigade, had surrounded Meiktila, which fell in four days. Almost the whole Japanese garrison, strongly dug in and amply provided with artillery and ammunition from the depots, was killed. The Japanese immediately counterattacked, and now the armored/mechanized columns were able to take toll of them in the open, so that a continuous series of battles was fought across the entire front. At the same time, Mandalay fell after much bitter street fighting. On Mandalay Hill, converted to a fortress and taken by British and Gurkhas in hand-to-hand fighting, the defenders had finally to be burned out by rolling drums of petrol into their bunkers and setting fire to them with tracer

Division, which started south as soon as Myitkyina had fallen in August 1944; but their efforts relaxed by mid-March and the Chinese were diverted home just as the main clash in central Burma was at its height. The XV Corps cleaned up the Arakan, but there was no way of developing its further thrust. It was thus the IV and XXXIII Corps of the 14th Army which took on the hard Japanese core and destroyed it.

The final battle for Burma was a complex affair, involving an advance up to and across the Chindwin; the secret move of the IV Corps, so that it arrived to threaten Meiktila from a totally unexpected direction; the crossing of the Irrawaddy, a river 1,750 yards (1600m) wide in places, with shifting sand banks and strong and treacherous currents, in four places along a distance of 150 miles (240km); a number of operations

bullets. A sign of the times, however, was that the ancient Fort Dufferin, the keep of the city and proof against heavy artillery and bombing, was tamely evacuated. By the end of March, the decisive battle of central Burma had been fought and won, and Slim was anxious to advance on Rangoon.

At this point there was almost a serious setback. The sudden withdrawal of the Chinese and U.S. forces in the north was tolerable, but what was totally unexpected was the decision to use the U.S. Army Air Forces' transport aircraft, hitherto at the disposal of the 14th Army, to ferry them out, which severely affected the whole mobility of the 14th Army. Fortunately, the Combined Chiefs of Staff Committee in the USA relented after appeals came from Admiral Lord Mountbatten, of the South-East Asia Command, and the British chiefs of staff in London. The diversion of the U.S. air transport facility was therefore delayed until June 1 or the fall of Rangoon, whichever was the earlier. In fact the real deadline was May 15, as the monsoon rains could be expected on that date, slowing or halting all armor and interfering with air operations. Thus Rangoon had to be taken in 40 days; there were 250 miles (400km) to be covered, as the crow flies, and Japanese resistance was strong.

Slim ordered the IV Corps to drive straight down the road from Meiktila to Rangoon down the valley of the Sittang river, with divisions leapfrogging past each other and armored battle groups leading without any regard for their flanks. They would get to Rangoon first

Admiral Lord Louis Mountbatten, the Allied commander-in-chief in South-East Asia, takes the salute during the victory parade in Rangoon, the capital of liberated Burma, in 1945.

OPPOSITE ABOVE: *A Japanese machine-gun team in Burma. By this time, though still full of fight, the Japanese in the Burma campaign were short of all necessities, even by their own spartan standards, including food, fuel, ammunition, and medicine.*

OPPOSITE BELOW: *Japanese infantry in China. By 1944, in the Chinese theater, the primary task of the Japanese armies was to capture food by overrunning areas as soon as the harvest had been gathered, and to take and hold the areas from which the U.S. Army Air Forces could launch Boeing B-29 Superfortress heavy bomber raids on Japan.*

and then turn back to mop up or consolidate, should any Japanese resistance flare up behind them. At the same time, at Slim's request, the "Dracula" seaborne operation was reduced in size so that it could be expedited and Rangoon attacked from the sea to coincide with the last stages of the land advance and thus pin any reserves. On the other, longer route to Rangoon down the valley of the Irrawaddy river through Prome, the XXXIII Corps was to advance from the west. The Japanese forces who attempted to come in from the east were checked by a resistance movement, carefully fostered in advance by the Karens, and by a technique developed in Burma by the Chindits: clandestine ground observers with radio sets calling for RAF attacks. By April 22 Slim's primary advance in the Sittang valley had reached Toungoo. On May 1, the day before Dracula was to be implemented, a reconnaissance aircraft over Rangoon saw painted on the roof of a jail, which was known to hold many British prisoners-of-war, the words: "Japs gone. Exdigitate"(RAF wartime slang meaning "pull your finger out").

The pilot of a de Havilland Mosquito had decided to land on Rangoon airfield, where he damaged his aircraft; he walked to Rangoon, hitched a lift downriver in a sampan, and brought the news that Rangoon was empty. The Japanese had indeed left in panic, and the landings were unopposed.

The Japanese had yet to surrender, however, and the last phase of the war was both cruel and unnecessary. For the field army surrender was impossible; in fact Japanese-speaking liaison officers could not persuade some to do so even after the order to cease-fire from the Emperor Hirohito himself had been broadcast from Tokyo: it was believed to be a propaganda trick. The surviving Japanese, without ammunition or supplies, were in the hilly tract of the Pegu Yomas, to the west of the IV Corps' route, and were now cordoned off by a belt of strongpoints down the road. The Japanese were ordered to break out and cross the dangerous Sittang river by raft, or by swimming, and then make for Thailand to continue the struggle. The weather was bad, the river in flood, many were ill and all were starving. The Japanese were shot down in very large numbers by the Indian 17th Division as they crossed the road, or from Bren gun posts along the banks when they were in the river. Many were drowned and many more killed by the villagers on the east bank. At last, a few survivors gave up.

WORLD WAR II
Chapter Eight
THE WAR IN CHINA

Japan's interest in China, principally as a market for its growing industries, extended from the later part of the 19th century. From 1931, however, Japan had stepped up its pressure in China, especially in the military sense. Various incidents in the 1930s culminated in the so-called Marco Polo Bridge Incident of July 7, 1937, when Chinese and Japanese troops clashed just outside Peking in an affair carefully engineered by the Japanese. Here, at last, was the excuse for which they had been waiting, and the Japanese wasted no time in launching a full-scale invasion of China.

Although Chiang Kai-shek's Chinese forces numbered some 2 million men, whose quality was poor, as were both leadership and weaponry. Chiang's main interest at this time, and in the years to come, was the problem of the Communist guerrilla forces of Mao Tse-tung, although the two sides in the civil war had nominally resolved their differences in the face of the foreign threat. The Japanese army, on the other hand, was a comparatively small but nonetheless formidable force, well-equipped and ably led, having great fighting ability and skill. Unlike the Chinese, moreover, the Japanese had excellent army and navy air forces, and these played important strategic and tactical roles until the advent of the American Volunteer Group checked their activities. China's most powerful weapon, it could be argued, was world opinion, or rather U.S. opinion, of the Japanese invasion, whose almost total condemnation led to a gradual increase in the supply of money and modern weapons to Chiang's government.

Initially, the Japanese had it all their own way. Between July and December 1937, forces from Manchuria made large gains to the north of the Yellow river. Large areas of Chahar and Suiyuan were taken, but the main effort went into a drive south down the railway toward Hankow, Nanking, and Sian. Civil unrest behind them, combined with problems of logistics, served to halt the drive of the Japanese North China Area Army in December, while farther to the south, the Japanese China Expeditionary Army attacked Shanghai on August 8. The Chinese put up a surprisingly effective resistance, and it was not until November 8 that the Japanese were able to clear the city. By the end of the year further reinforcements had allowed the army to move inland along the line of the Yangtze river to take Nanking, the Chinese capital, by December 13. By the end of the year, therefore, Japan had taken two large and strategically important areas of China. With Chiang's attention drawn more to this threat than to themselves, the Communists had also profited, securing most of north-west China for themselves. Nevertheless, it should be noted that the Communists' 8th Route Army, under the command of the able Chu Teh, had been helping the nationalist cause considerably with raids on the Japanese. Indeed, in the only major battle against the Japanese fought by the Communists on September 25, the 8th Route Army's 115th Division

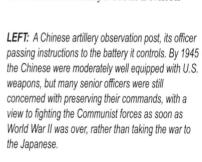

LEFT: A Chinese artillery observation post, its officer passing instructions to the battery it controls. By 1945 the Chinese were moderately well equipped with U.S. weapons, but many senior officers were still concerned with preserving their commands, with a view to fighting the Communist forces as soon as World War II was over, rather than taking the war to the Japanese.

OPPOSITE: Chinese infantry in action.

had ambushed and cut to pieces the Japanese 5th Division in the Battle of P'inghsinkuan in northern Shansi.

On December 12, the Japanese made a grave strategic error in dive-bombing British and U.S. gunboats on the Yangtze river, and sinking the American vessel *Panay*. The attack was quite unprovoked, and caused enormous British and U.S. anger. Although Japan immediately paid a large indemnity, U.S. public opinion was now even more firmly against the Japanese.

Determined to link their two areas of control, the Japanese launched renewed offensives in January 1938. The North China Area Army struck south again after securing all of Shantung, and although its progress was steady, a nasty surprise lay in wait. During April, some 60,000 Japanese were cut off at Taierchwang by 200,000 Chinese under General Li Tsung-jen. After a desperate struggle, the Japanese hacked their way out to the north again, but only at the cost of 20,000 dead. After a swift regrouping, the North China Area Army renewed its advance in May, taking Kaifeng by June 6. By the end of the month, the whole of the rail line between Nanking and Peking was in Japanese hands. Then, advancing west from Kaifeng to take the key junction of Chengchow, on the Hankow railway, the Japanese were rebuffed when the Chinese breached the Yellow river dykes, flooding large areas and causing the Japanese to lose many men and much matériel. The offensive was cancelled in July.

The Japanese then shifted their main line of advance further south, and once again made progress toward Chiang's capital of Hankow. The city finally fell after bloody fighting on October 25. Chiang again moved his capital, this time to Chungking, farther up the Yangtze river in the province of Szechwan.

On October 12, meanwhile, the 23rd Army, part of the 6th Area Army, had landed near Hong Kong, moving quickly on Canton, China's most important port after Shanghai. Canton fell on October 21, but the Japanese then felt it necessary to reconsider their overall strategy. It was now decided that instead of the rapid

advances of the previous 18 months, a war of attrition would be waged. With civil unrest and guerrilla operations rife in the areas they had conquered, the Japanese considered additional conquests futile, and instead decided to concentrate on destroying Chiang's forces wherever they could be found. Only after the Chinese armies had been destroyed, the Japanese felt, could the rest of China be occupied and pacified. In 1939, therefore, the Japanese confined themselves to securing a number of ports previously left untouched between Shanghai and Canton, taking the island of Hainan, and straightening their line in the Hankow and Wuchow regions of central China.

Activities in 1940 were limited to the Communists' so-called "100 Regiments Offensive" between August 30 and November 30, when guerrillas attacked Japanese posts in Shansi, Chahar, Hopeh, and Honan, disrupting the Japanese rear areas very successfully. For their part, the Japanese devoted 1940 to Indochina, which they began to

occupy in September. This proved to be the first link in the chain of events that was to take Japan to war with the USA. In 1941, the Japanese launched a series of reprisal raids for the 100 Regiments Offensive. The series continued into 1943, costing the Communists some 100,000 dead. Now, preoccupied with the events that had led it to a world war, Japan's activities in China slumped considerably.

The year 1942 was also marked by the continued lull in operations, with Japanese attention turned toward the consolidation of her conquests in South-East Asia and in the Pacific. The Japanese, therefore, remained on the defensive in China, and Chiang confined his efforts to supporting the British in Burma. For only here, via Rangoon and the Burma Road, could American matériel aid reach him. Within China, acute command problems were arising between Brigadier-General Claire L. Chennault, commanding the China Air Task Force (lately the American Volunteer Group), and Lieutenant-

General Joseph W. Stilwell, Chiang's chief of staff and military adviser. With the cutting of the Burma Road and the institution of the airlift of supplies "over the hump" of the eastern Himalayas, there were not enough supplies to go round. Concerned with the security of China on land, Stilwell wanted the supplies for the Chinese army, while Chennault, on the other hand, who considered that the war could only be taken to the Japanese by his growing air power, requested priority for his own needs. The eventual allocations satisfied neither party, although as Stilwell had believed in a near parity of supplies for each party, he was the better satisfied.

In 1943, China's position was desperate, its isolation from western sources of supply having profound effects on its armed forces. Had the Japanese been interested in major offensives, the Chinese would have found it hard, perhaps even impossible, to check them. But the Japanese were content to launch the first of their series of "rice offensives." With many of their combat veterans transferred to active theaters, the Japanese armies in China now had large numbers of raw recruits. The rice offensives, which were local attacks with

limited objectives, were an ideal means of blooding them. The idea behind the offensives was for the Japanese to drive into a hitherto untouched area of China after the rice crop had just been harvested. The Japanese would advance swiftly, seize the harvest to feed themselves, and then pull back. In one of these offensives, however, the Japanese suffered a sharp rebuff at the Battle of Changteh, when U.S. air support enabled the Chinese to throw the Japanese back in an action that lasted from 23 November 23 to December 9. Roosevelt, meanwhile, who had been the arbitrator in the Chennault-Stilwell controversy in favor of the former, was now promoted to major-general and appointed to the command of the new 14th Army Air Force in China. Chennault was thus able to increase the scope of his attacks on the Japanese rear areas. Chiang's efforts in 1943 were restricted mainly to the establishment of a blockade of the Communist-controlled areas of north-west China, despite the truce between the two parties.

In 1944, the Chinese Communists and the Japanese came to an unofficial truce, although it is still not known whether this was negotiated or merely

allowed to happen. The result was that the Japanese were able to deploy troops from this area in more important zones, and the Communists were able to consolidate yet further their hold on north-west China. Most of the Japanese forces from the north were shifted south for an offensive against Chennault's airfields. Built by hundreds of thousands of Chinese coolies, these were now

ABOVE LEFT: Many armed elements in China were less well equipped with modern U.S. weapons, these men having a miscellany of captured weapons and even, in the foreground, a locally made black-powder weapon.

ABOVE: Chinese Communist soldiers with Japanese Type 97 medium tanks, probably supplied by the Soviets from the stocks they had captured in Manchuria, or possibly seized from the failing Japanese forces in China.

OPPOSITE: Mao Tse-tung, the leader of the Communist movement in China, was ultimately the victor in the civil war which was resumed after the surrender of Japan.

numerous and well placed to make strategically significant raids on Japanese positions as far afield as Formosa and Manchuria. The most important of these bases were Nanning, Liuchow, Kweilin, Lingling, Hengyang, and Chihkiang, all but the last being on the old Hanoi to Changsha railway, and at Laohokow and Ankang on the upper Han Chiang river. The Japanese now decided that these must be eliminated, the northern pair by an attack from Kaifeng, and the southern bases by a three-pronged offensive from Indochina in the south, Canton in the east, and Changsha in the north-east. Throughout the period from January to May 1944, the Japanese planned their offensives carefully and gathered supplies. At the same time, General Yasuji Okamura's China Expeditionary Army undertook a series of attacks intended to clear the railways of north-east China of the guerrillas plaguing them and so ease the problems of the Japanese logistical staffs.

Not foreseeing what was to come, Chiang allowed Stilwell to use the best Chinese formations for an offensive in Burma, starting in May. Four days before this Chinese Yunnan offensive started on May 11, the Japanese launched their east China offensive. In fierce fighting the Japanese advanced steadily against patchy opposition. Most of Chennault's airfields were lost by the end of November, by which time the Chinese position was desperate. The Yunnan offensive in Burma was called off and the two best divisions flown back to China by U.S. aircraft. Chiang, whose relations with Stilwell had been poor for some time, finally had him replaced by Major-General Albert C. Wedemeyer on October 18. Wedemeyer reorganized the Chinese defense, and in a counteroffensive east of Kweiyang on December 10, finally brought the Japanese to a halt.

In January and February 1945, however, the Japanese again went over to the offensive in south-east China, making great conquests on each side of the Hanoi to Hankow railway. In March, the offensive was extended into central China, and the region between

the Yangtze and Yellow rivers was seized, together with its major rice crop. For the Americans, the important airbase at Laohokow was a major loss when it fell on April 8 after a sterling defense beginning on March 26. The Chinese counterattacked on April 10, halting this central offensive, and later managed to do the same with renewed offensives against Changteh and Chihkiang. With the tide of war now running very strongly against them, the Japanese realized they were overextended in China, particularly at the expense of the Kwantung Army in Manchuria, where the Soviets were now looking distinctly threatening. From May onwards Okamura began to pull in his horns and rationalize his positions. He was not fast enough. Chinese offensives had cut the Japanese links with Indochina by the end of May. The Chinese offensives continued, and by the beginning of July some 100,000 Japanese troops were cooped up inside a defensive perimeter at Canton. Ably supported by U.S. air power, the Chinese drove north-east, pushing the Japanese before them toward Kaifeng, the great airfield complex at Kweilin falling back into Allied hands on July 27. The Chinese drove on into August, when the armistice came, and the

Japanese laid down their arms, most of which were gladly seized by Mao's Communists and Chiang's nationalists. With the Japanese threat removed, the Chinese civil war was resumed in full.

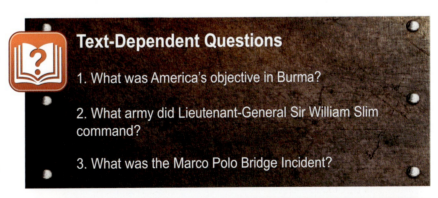

Text-Dependent Questions

1. What was America's objective in Burma?

2. What army did Lieutenant-General Sir William Slim command?

3. What was the Marco Polo Bridge Incident?

Research Projects

Summarize China's role in World War II.

WORLD WAR II

Chapter Nine
THE SOVIET WAR AGAINST JAPAN

The Soviets and Japanese had signed a Non-Aggression Treaty on April 13, 1941, yet just under three-and-a-half years later Soviet forces were to invade Manchukuo (the Japanese puppet state of Manchuria) as well as Inner Mongolia and Korea and even parts of Japan, in the form of the southern half of Sakhalin Island and the Kurile Islands group. The reason was quite simply that the USSR wished to regain the portions of the tsarist empire lost in the Russo-Japanese War of 1904–05. At the Yalta Conference of February 1945, between Churchill, Roosevelt, and Stalin, the two western leaders agreed to the USSR's ambitions in the east if they entered the war against Japan within three months of the conclusion of the war against Germany.

The UK and USA wished for Soviet intervention so that Japan's forces would be yet further weakened before the Allies launched the great invasion of Japan planned for November 1945; and Soviet intervention was almost certainly sure to destroy Japan's Kwantung Army.

A large part of Japan's heavy industry was based in Manchukuo, and it was from here that Japan's invasion of northern China in 1937 had started. At its peak, the Kwantung Army had been a mighty force, but relative peace on this front, coupled with the constant and growing demands from other fronts as the war progressed, meant that the best formations and equipment had been bled off to supply the needs of other Japanese forces. In the middle of 1945 the Kwantung Army was still formidable on paper, but its matériel was obsolete, and its under-strength divisions were mostly manned by reservists.

For his invasion, however, Stalin assembled powerful forces, with the best of modern equipment, and men and commanders well versed in the techniques of modern mobile warfare

after the war with Germany. Three large fronts, or army groups, were gathered for the offensive, although only two were to play major roles. West of Manchuria was Marshal R.Y. Malinovsky's Trans-Baikal Front of five armies, one of them a tank army. These would strike south toward

Peking in China, and south-east toward Tsitsihar, Harbin and Changchun. During their south-east thrust the armies of the Trans-Baikal Front were to link up in Manchuria with the armies of Marshal K.A. Meretskov's 1st Far East Front, striking west with four armies

OPPOSITE: The history of Russian and Soviet rivalry with the Japanese in eastern Asia, extending back into the latter part of the 19th century, saw a Japanese victory in the Russo-Japanese War of 1904–05, which settled into an armed neutrality after a succession of border clashes, some of them sizeable, in 1938–39. These are Japanese troops in action on the disputed border with the USSR in 1939.

BELOW: Before entering the war against Japan, the Soviet armies had rested and rebuilt the strength of their Far Eastern forces with armies and other formations that were of very high combat capability after their defeat of the Germans.

from eastern Siberia. In the north was the 2nd Far East Front, under General M.A. Purkaev, which was to take the great northern bulge of Manchuria, only lightly held by the Japanese. Other formations of the 1st Far East Front, notably the 16th Army, were to invade the Japanese southern half of Sakhalin Island from the north. Finally, a mixed force of marines and infantry was to invade and take the Kurile Islands from Kamchatka, with the aid of the Pacific Fleet. Overall command was exercised by Marshal A.M. Vasilevsky, and once the Trans-Baikal and 1st Far East Fronts had linked, the Soviets were to drive on Port Arthur, one of the most important objectives of the campaign.

On the whole, the problems the

Soviets were due to face were geographical and climatic, especially in the west, where Malinovsky's forces would have to cross large parts of the waterless Gobi Desert. But in the east, on the Ussuri river front, the Japanese had long realized that in a war with the USSR this area would be very vulnerable, and had accordingly built fixed fortifications in great depth. To deal with these, the Soviets deployed forces experienced in dealing with German fixed defences.

Two days after the first atomic bomb was dropped on Hiroshima on August 6, 1945, the USSR declared war on Japan. The powerful air forces, gathered for the Manchurian campaign, struck out at Japanese targets as the armies rolled over

the frontiers swiftly and irresistibly, with the exception of some of the 1st Far East Front's formations. On the Mongolian front, the Japanese fell back in good order and dug in on the slopes of the Khingan mountain range. But Malinovsky's armor burst through in the south, outflanking the more northern Japanese positions. Thereafter, the Soviets pressed on swiftly and ruthlessly, crushing or bypassing Japanese centers of resistance to ensure the greatest speed. Changchun had fallen by August 20, as had Mukden. The 6th Guards Tank Army rolled on to Port Arthur, which fell on August 22. The lightning advance of these forces had broken the back and the will of the Kwantung Army, in a display of dazzling mobile warfare rarely seen before or since. Great credit must go to

the Soviet air forces, which kept the tanks supplied with fuel and the men with water and food.

Farther to the south, others of Malinovsky's forces had struck down through the Gobi Desert toward Kalgan and Chengteh, the latter falling on August 18, which allowed the Soviets to press on to the coast. Both Kalgan and Chengteh were taken with the aid of the Chinese Communist 8th People's Army.

In the east, Meretskov's forces initially had considerable trouble with the fixed defenses between Lake Khanga and the sea, the Japanese even going so far as to launch counterattacks which the Soviets found very dangerous. By August 14, however, the 1st Far East Front had broken through the fortifications and appalling terrain to

ABOVE: *A Soviet cavalry patrol on the border between Outer Mongolia and Manchuria, the latter being a Japanese puppet kingdom otherwise known as Manchukuo.*

OPPOSITE ABOVE: *A Japanese cavalry patrol in an occupied part of Inner Mongolia.*

OPPOSITE BELOW: *After the Soviet victory in the lightning war against the Japanese in eastern Asia, the defeated Japanese were set to work on tasks such as leveling the border defenses by filling in antitank ditches and the like.*

open country. The advance on Harbin now got under way in earnest. Aided by the Pacific Fleet, operating from Vladivostok, the Soviet land forces were also probing far into Korea, the 2nd Far East Front in the far north was making steady progress against moderate opposition, and the 16th Army was moving well down into Sakhalin.

On August 14, the Japanese surrendered unconditionally, but not the slightest notice was taken of it by the Soviets, who were determined to secure all their objectives before halting. The Soviets claim, however, was that in defiance of their government's surrender order, many Japanese units, especially in the Kirin and Harbin areas, continued to offer stiff resistance. On August 17, the commander of the Kwantung Army got in touch with Vasilevsky and attempted to arrange a cease-fire, but the Soviet commander refused on the grounds that Japanese forces were still fighting after the previous surrender. The reason was probably that Japanese communications had broken down and the relevant formations did not know of the surrender, or if they did, their commanders had ordered them to fight on regardless. The major industrial city of Harbin was taken by the 1st Far East Front on August 18, while the Soviet advance continued apace elsewhere. By the time all the Japanese forces in Manchuria had laid down their arms on August 27, the Soviets had seized all of their objectives.

Any assessment of the campaign must take into account the weakness of the Japanese, but the Soviets' performance was nonetheless a staggering one. Battle-wise and tough, they had clearly learned much from the Germans' manifest ability with armored and mobile forces. Although these casualty figures are probably too low, it cannot be by too much, with 8,219 dead and 22,264 wounded. The Soviets also claim to have killed 83,737 Japanese, wounded an unknown number, and taken at least 600,000 prisoners. Most of the latter were shipped off to the USSR and, as with many of the USSR's German prisoners, a great number were never seen outside the USSR again.

If the performance of the Soviets was good, that of the Japanese was odd. Even allowing for the fact that it was at the end of the war, and that morale was low, some units had quite uncharacteristically given up without a fight. Other formations, however, continued to fight showing the old Japanese bravura despite the obsolescence of their equipment and the poor physical condition of most of the men.

At minimal cost, the USSR had secured for itself a vast slice of eastern Asia, together with an excellent year-round port.

WORLD WAR II

Chapter Ten
THE ATOMIC BOMBINGS OF HIROSHIMA AND NAGASAKI

With the conquest of Okinawa completed, the Americans were faced with the appalling prospect of invading Japan. Plans were drawn up for Operation Olympic as a series of 6th Army landings on Kyushu on November 1, 1945 and for Operation Coronet as a series of 1st and 8th Army landings on Honshu on March 1, 1945. Judging by past performances, the Japanese would put up a powerful and fanatical defense, and American planners estimated that the invasion forces would suffer at least 1 million casualties before the back of the defence was broken. What else could the Americans do? It seemed unlikely that the Japanese would surrender unconditionally, and so the Allies would have to invade the Japanese home islands in order to bring the Pacific war to a successful conclusion.

Unknown to all but a very few high-ranking officers and politicians, another solution was being worked upon. For some time, the possibilities of using radioactive materials for explosive purposes had been suspected, and a large

ABOVE: *U.S. Army poster prepares the public for the invasion of Japan after ending war on Germany and Italy.*

LEFT: *The mushroom cloud rises over Hiroshima on August 9, 1945 after the explosion of the world's second atomic bomb.*

OPPOSITE: *The Nagasaki mushroom cloud.*

team of Allied scientists had spent a great part of the war trying to develop a weapon based on uranium or plutonium. At last, the scientists were ready for their first practical test at Alamogordo in New Mexico. An atomic device was triggered by remote control on July 16, 1945 and a light "brighter than a thousand suns" burst over the desert. Seconds later an enormous blast shook the ground and the air. The atomic bomb was feasible.

The problem for Harry S. Truman, who had become president of the USA on the death of Franklin D. Roosevelt on April 12, 1945, was to decide whether or not to use the new weapon. The bomb was there, and so was the means to deliver it in the form of the 509th Composite Group, USAAF, which had

OPPOSITE ABOVE: The "Fat Man" was the 21-kiloton atomic bomb dropped on Nagasaki on August 9, 1945. This was an implosion-type weapon with a plutonium core, whereas the 13–16-kiloton "Little Man" bomb dropped on Hiroshima was a gun-type weapon with a uranium core.

OPPOSITE BELOW: Seen on returning to its base on the Mariana Islands group after its mission, the B-29, named Enola Gay, was the bomber which dropped the atomic bomb on Hiroshima.

ABOVE: The devastation in Nagasaki, some 880 yards (805m) from ground zero, the point on the ground 1,540ft (469m) below the bomb's aerial detonation.

RIGHT: This wristwatch, recovered from Hiroshima, stopped at the moment of the first atomic bomb's detonation, shortly after 8:15am on August 6, 1945.

been training in the deserts of Utah with its Boeing B-29 Superfortress bombers. The debate was heated, but in the end most senior commanders consulted, and Secretary of War Henry L. Stimson, thought that the new weapon should be used. Japan still had enormous military strength, they reasoned, and why should U.S. lives be lost in their hundreds of thousands when a means of preventing this was available? Truman agreed with reluctance. At the Potsdam Conference in July, Truman told Clement Attlee, the British prime minister in succession to Winston Churchill, about the weapon and his decision to use it. In the Potsdam Declaration of July 7 Truman and Attlee called on Japan to surrender, warning that refusal to do so would entail the "inevitable and complete destruction of the Japanese armed forces and . . . the

utter devastation of the Japanese homeland." When Japan failed to reply, Truman gave his authority for the first atomic bomb to be dropped.

The target selected was Hiroshima, a city of some 300,000 people, which was an important military objective but, as yet, little affected by conventional attacks. On August 6 a B-29, named *Enola Gay* after the mother of its pilot, Colonel Paul Tibbetts, took off from the Marianas and headed for Japan. The air-raid warning was sounded in Hiroshima, but seeing that there were only a few planes overhead, most people failed to take cover. The bomb was dropped, and exploded at exactly the intended place and height, with a force equal to that of the detonation of between 13,000 and 16,000 tons of TNT. Exact figures are still not available, but it seems that 78,150 people died almost immediately and another 70,000 were injured. Most of the center of Hiroshima was completely destroyed.

The impact of the bomb on Japanese politicians and military leaders was profound but at the same time was viewed with incredulity. The dropping of a second bomb on Nagasaki, on August 9, altered that and convinced Japan's leaders that the war must end. The Nagasaki explosion, of some 21 kilotons, killed 40,000 and injured 25,000 people out of a population of some 250,000. Luckily for the Japanese, the country on which the city is built is hilly, and this diverted much of the blast.

The Emperor Hirohito at last made a firm decision and insisted on peace. There were inevitably dissenters, and a coup had to be put down in Tokyo.

OPPOSITE ABOVE: *The devastation in Nagasaki, some 880 yards (805m) from ground zero, the point on the ground 1,540 feet (469m) below the bomb's aerial detonation, was exactly halfway between the Mitsubishi steel and arms works in the south and the Mitsubishi-Urakami torpedo factory in the north.*

BELOW: *The Japanese surrender delegation on board the U.S. Navy's battleship* Missouri *in Tokyo Bay on September 2, 1945.*

Following discussions by radio, Japan agreed to an unconditional surrender, which in fact had several conditions for the benefit of the Japanese: the emperor was to remain, and Japan also was to remain undivided.

A cease-fire came into effect on August 15, although many Japanese refused to believe the emperor's broadcast and fought on for a few more days. They imagined it to be an Allied trick, for none of them had ever heard the emperor's voice before, so great had been his apolitical seclusion. Gradually, however, peace fell over the battlefields of the Pacific and Asia during the next few days. On August 28 General Douglas MacArthur and the first U.S. occupation forces arrived in Japan, and the real impact of defeat began to be felt by the average Japanese. The formal end of the war against Japan came on September 2, in a ceremony on board the battleship *Missouri* in Tokyo Bay.

Now that about 50 million people had lost their lives, World War II was at last over

WORLD WAR II
TIME LINE OF WORLD WAR II

1939
Germany invades Poland on September 1.

Two days later Britain and France declare war on Germany.

1940
Rationing starts in the UK.

German "Blitzkrieg" overwhelms and overpowers Belgium, Holland, and France.

Churchill becomes Prime Minister of Britain.

British Expeditionary Force evacuated from Dunkirk.

Britain is victorious in the Battle of Britain. Hitler to postpones invasion plans.

1941
Operation Barbarossa commences – the invasion of Russia begins.

The Blitz continues against Britain. Major cities are badly damaged.

Allies take Tobruk in North Africa, and resist German attacks.

Japan attacks Pearl Harbor, and the U.S. enters the war.

1942
Germany suffers setbacks at Stalingrad and El Alamein.

Singapore falls to the Japanese in February – around 25,000 prisoners taken.

American naval victory at Battle of Midway, in June, marks turning point in Pacific War.

Mass murder of Jewish people at Auschwitz begins.

1943
Germany surrenders at Stalingrad. Germany's first major defeat.

The Allies are victorious in North Africa The invasion of Italy is launched.

Italy surrenders to the Allies, but Germany takes over the fight.

British and Indian forces fight Japanese in Burma.

1944
Allies land at Anzio and bomb monastery at Monte Cassino.

Soviet offensive gathers pace in Eastern Europe.

D-Day: The Allied invasion of France. Paris is liberated in August.

Guam liberated by the U.S. *Okinawa*, and Iwo Jima bombed.

1945
Auschwitz liberated by Soviet troops. Russians reach Berlin. Hitler commits suicide and Germany surrenders on May 7.

Truman becomes President of the U.S. on Roosevelt's death.

Attlee replaces Churchill.

After atomic bombs are dropped on Hiroshima and Nagasaki, Japan surrenders on August 14.

OPPOSITE: *The Sannō Shrine, located about 800 meters south-east of the atomic bomb hypocenter in Nagasaki, is noted for its one-legged stone torii at the shrine entrance.*

Series Glossary of Key Terms

Allied Powers A coalition of nations that fought against the Axis powers.

ANZAC An Australian or New Zealand soldier.

Appeasement A policy of agreeing to hostile demands in order to maintain peace.

Aryan In Nazi ideology, a Caucasian especially of Nordic type.

Auschwitz An industrial town in Poland and site of Nazi concentration camp during World War II.

Axis Powers An alignment of nations that fought against the Allied forces in World War II.

Blitzkrieg A surprise and violent offensive by air and ground forces.

Concentration camp A camp where prisoners of war are detained or confined.

D-Day June 6, 1944. The Allied invasion of France in World War II began.

Fascism A political movement or philosophy that exalts nation and race above the individual with an autocratic government and a dictator as leader.

Führer A leader or tyrant.

Final Solution The Nazi program to exterminate all the Jews throughout Europe.

Gestapo A secret-police employing devious ways of controlling people considered disloyal.

Holocaust The mass slaughter of European civilians especially the Jews by the Nazis during World War II.

Kamikaze A Japanese pilot trained to make suicidal crash attacks upon ships in World War II.

Lebensraum Territory considered necessary by Nazis for national existence.

Luftwaffe German air force.

Maginot Line Defensive fortifications on the eastern border of France during World War II.

Manhattan Project The code name for the secret U.S. project set up in 1942 to develop an atomic bomb.

Nazi An advocate of policies characteristic of Nazism.

Pact of Steel A military alliance between Nazi Germany and Fascist Italy concluded on May 22, 1939.

Panzer A German tank.

Potsdam Conference A conference held in Potsdam in the summer of 1945 where Roosevelt, Stalin, and Churchill drew up plans for the adminstration of Germany and Poland after World War II ended.

U-boat A German submarine especially in World War I and II.

The Versailles Treaty The treaty imposed on Germany by the Alllied powers in 1920 after the end of World War I.

Yalta Conference A conference held in Yalta in February 1945, where Roosevelt, Stalin, and Churchill planned the finals statge of World War II and agreed to new boundaries and territorial division in Europe.

Further Reading and Internet Resources

WEBSITES

http://www.bbc.co.uk/history/worldwars/wwtwo

http://www.history.com/topics/world-war-ii

https://www.britannica.com/event/World-War-II

http://www.world-war-2.info/

BOOKS

Hourly History. *World War II The Definitive Visual Guide.* Oxford University Press, 2010

Richard Overy. *The New York Times Complete World War II: The Coverage of the Entire Conflict.* 2016

Smithsonian. *World War II The Definitive Visual Guide* DK Publishing Inc., 2015.

If you enjoyed this book take a look at Mason Crest's other war series:

The Civil War, The Vietnam War, Major U.S. Historical Wars.

In this book, page numbers in ***bold italic font*** indicate photos or videos.

A

Adachi, Hotaze, 12

air force

atomic bombs, *5, 66–70,* 66–71, *73*

bombing campaigns, *6,* 50–53, *50–53*

British, 55, 57

Burma battles, 41, 55, 57

Central Pacific campaigns, 19–20, 21, 22, 26–27, 28–32, *29*

China battles, 59–60, 61

Indian, 41

Iwo Jima and Okinawa campaigns, 45–49

Japanese, *2, 13,* 19, 21, 22, 27, *29,* 29–32, 34, 36, 43, 47–49, 51–52, 53, 55

kamikaze pilots, *2, 29,* 43, 47, 48–49

parachute divisions, 14, 15, 41, 44

Philippines battles, 28, 34, 36–37, 43–44

Solomon Islands and New Guinea battles, 12, *13,* 14–15, *16,* 17

Soviet, 63–64

US, *6,* 12, 14, 15, *16,* 17, 19–20, 26–27, 28, 29–32, 34, 36–37, 43–44, 45–47, 49, 50–53, *50–53,* 57, 59–60, 61

Akiyama, Monzo, 21

Allied Powers

bombing campaigns, *6,* 50–53, *50–53* (*see also* atomic bombs)

Burma battles, *20,* 24–25, *24–25,* 38–41, *38–41,* 54–57, *54–57*

Central Pacific campaigns, 18–23, *18–23, 26–31,* 26–32

China battles, *56,* 58–61, *58–61*

Iwo Jima and Okinawa campaigns, 36, 45–49, *45–49*

Philippines battles, 28, *30, 32–36,* 33–37, *42–44,* 42–45

Solomon Islands and New Guinea battles, 12–17, *12–17*

Soviet war with Japan, 62–65, *62–65*

See also specific countries

armistice. *See* Japan: surrender of

atomic bombs, *5, 66–70,* 66–71, *73*

Attlee, Clement, 69

Australia, Solomon Islands and New Guinea battles, 13–14, 16–17

B

Barbey, Daniel E., 37

Battle of Leyte Gulf, *30,* 33–35, *35,* 37

Battle of the Philippine Sea, 29–32, *30–31*

Battles of Imphal and Kohima, 38–41, *38–41*

Belleau Wood, 2, 32

Blarney, Thomas, 14, 17

Bogan, G. F., 33–34

bombing campaigns, *6,* 50–53, *50–53*

See also atomic bombs

Bruce, Andrew D., 28, 48

Buckner, Simon Bolivar, 47, 48, 49

Burma battles, *20,* 24–25, *24–25,* 38–41, *38–41,* 54–57, *54–57*

C

Canada, Central Pacific campaigns, 23

casualties

British, 25, 54

Chinese, 59

Filipino, 44

Japanese, 14, 17, 19, 20–21, *26,* 28, 29, 31, 37, 41, 44–45, 46, 49, 53, 65, 70

Soviet, 65

US, 17, 20–21, 23, *26,* 28, 29, 32, 37, 44–45, 46, 49

Cates, Clifton B., 29, 46

cavalry, 12, 13, 16, 37, 44, *64–65*

Central Pacific campaigns, 18–23, *18–23, 26–31,* 26–32

Chennault, Claire L., 50, 59–60, 61

Chiang Kai-shek, 25, 50, 58–60, 61

China

battles in, *56,* 58–61, *58–61*

bombing campaigns based in, *6,* 50–51

Burma battles, 24–25, 40, 41, 55–56

China Air Task Force, 50, 59–60

Chinese Army in India (CAI), 24–25, 40, 41, 55

Communist forces, *58,* 58–61, *60–61,* 64

Soviet aid from, 64

Churchby, Gerald, *8*

Churchill, Winston, 62

Chu Teh, 58

code breaking or cryptanalysis, 19, 22

Cowan, D. T., 56

D

Davison, R. E., 33–34

E

Eichelberger, Robert L., 43

Enola Gay, 68, 70

Erskine, Graves B., 46

G

Geiger, Roy S., 27, 36, 47

Giffard, Henry, 41

Gilbert Islands battles, *3,* 20–21

Griner, George W., 27

Griswold, Oscar W., 15, 43

Guam battles, *19, 20,* 26, 28, *28,* 30, 31

H

Hale, Willis H., 20

Hall, Charles P., 43

Halsey, William F., 12–13, 14, 16, 18, 19, 33–34, 35, 36–37, 43, 46

Herring, Edmund F., 13

Hester, John P., 15

Hirohito, Emperor, 57, 70–71

Hiroshima, atomic bombing of, *5, 66,* 66–71, *68–69*

Hodge, John B., 37, 47

Hosogaya, Boshiro, 22–23

I

Imamura, Hitoshi, 12

OPPOSITE: *Commodore Perry's flag was flown from Annapolis, Maryland to Tokyo for display at the surrender ceremonies which officially ended World War II.*

PHOTOGRAPHIC ACKNOWLEDGEMENTS

All images in this book are supplied by Cody Images and are in the public domain.

The contents of this book was first published as *WORLD WAR II*.

ABOUT THE AUTHOR
Christopher Chant

Christopher Chant is a successful writer on aviation and modern military matters, and has a substantial number of authoritative titles to his credit. He was born in Cheshire, England in December 1945, and spent his childhood in East Africa, where his father was an officer in the Colonial Service. He returned to the UK for his education at the King's School, Canterbury (1959–64) and at Oriel College, Oxford (1964–68). Aviation in particular and military matters in general have long been a passion, and after taking his degree he moved to London as an assistant editor on the Purnell partworks, *History of the Second World War* (1968–69) and *History of the First World War* (1969–72). On completion of the latter he moved to Orbis Publishing as editor of the partwork, *World War II* (1972–74), on completion of which he decided to become a freelance writer and editor.

Living first in London, then in Lincolnshire after his marriage in 1978, and currently in Sutherland, at the north-western tip of Scotland, he has also contributed as editor and writer to the partworks, *The Illustrated Encyclopedia of Aircraft*, *War Machine*, *Warplane*, *Take-Off*, *World Aircraft Information Files* and *World Weapons*, and to the magazine *World Air Power Journal*. In more recent years he was also involved in the creation of a five-disk CR-ROM series, covering the majority of the world's military aircraft from World War I to the present, and also in the writing of scripts for a number of video cassette and TV programs, latterly for Continuo Creative.

As sole author, Chris has more than 90 books to his credit, many of them produced in multiple editions and co-editions, including more than 50 on aviation subjects. As co-author he has contributed to 15 books, ten of which are also connected with aviation. He has written the historical narrative and technical database for a five-disk *History of Warplanes* CD-ROM series, and has been responsible for numerous video cassette programs on military and aviation matters, writing scripts for several TV programmes and an A–Z 'All the World's Aircraft' section in Aerospace/Bright Star *World Aircraft Information Files* partwork. He has been contributing editor to a number of books on naval, military and aviation subjects as well as to numerous partworks concerned with military history and technology. He has also produced several continuity card sets on aircraft for publishers such as Agostini, Del Prado, Eaglemoss, Edito-Service and Osprey.